THINK LIKE A
WARRIOR

<u>Books by Darrin Donnelly</u>

THINK LIKE A WARRIOR
The Five Inner Beliefs That Make You Unstoppable

OLD SCHOOL GRIT
Times May Change, But the Rules for Success Never Do

RELENTLESS OPTIMISM
How a Commitment to Positive Thinking Changes Everything

LIFE TO THE FULLEST
A Story About Finding Your Purpose and Following Your Heart

VICTORY FAVORS THE FEARLESS
How to Defeat the 7 Fears That Hold You Back

THINK LIKE A
WARRIOR

The Five Inner Beliefs That Make You Unstoppable

Darrin Donnelly

Copyright © 2016 by Darrin Donnelly.
All rights reserved.

Published in the United States by Shamrock New Media, Inc.

All rights reserved. No part of this publication may be reproduced in any form by any means, in whole or in part, without the prior written consent of Shamrock New Media, Inc. This includes reprints, excerpts, photocopying, recording, or any other means of reproducing text. If you would like to do any of the above, please seek permission by contacting the publisher at: info@shamrocknewmedia.com

Limit of Liability/Disclaimer of Warranty: This publication contains statements and statistics believed to be reliable, but neither the author(s) nor the publisher can guarantee the accuracy or completeness of any of the information contained in this publication. No warranty is made with respect to the accuracy or completeness of the information contained herein. The strategies outlined in this publication may not be suitable for every individual, and are not guaranteed or warranted to produce any particular results. The author(s) and publisher specifically disclaim any responsibility for any liability, loss, or risk, personal or otherwise, which is incurred as a consequence, directly or indirectly, of the use and application of any of the contents of this publication.

This book is a work of fiction. The names, characters, places, organizations, and events are either products of the author's imagination or used fictitiously to enhance the setting.

Unless specifically stated elsewhere, this book is not officially associated with, endorsed by, affiliated with, or sponsored by any of the individuals, entities, companies, or organizations written about in this book.

Cover design by Damonza.

ISBN-13: 978-0692705469
ISBN-10: 0692705465

Visit us at: SportsForTheSoul.com

Sports for the Soul

This book is part of the *Sports for the Soul* series. For updates on this book, a sneak peek at future books, and a free newsletter that delivers powerful advice and inspiration from top coaches, athletes, and sports psychologists, join us at: **SportsForTheSoul.com**.

The *Sports for the Soul* newsletter will help you:
- Find your purpose and follow your passion
- Use a positive mental attitude to achieve more
- Build your self-confidence
- Develop mental toughness
- Increase your energy and stay motivated
- Harness the power of positive self-talk
- Explore the spiritual side of success
- Be a positive leader for your family and your team
- Become the best version of yourself
- And much more…

Join us now at **SportsForTheSoul.com**. It's inspiring, it's life-changing, and it's FREE!

To Laura, Patrick, Katie, and Tommy;
who are everything to me.

And to John, Buck, Herb, Paul, and Vince;
whose timeless words of wisdom continue to inspire us.

Introduction

Success is a choice. Whether you succeed or fail is primarily determined by the beliefs you *choose* to hold about yourself and the world around you.

Numerous studies confirm that a person's mindset determines the type of life a person lives. Whether you are happy and successful or frustrated and miserable is a result of your mindset. And your mindset is determined by your inner beliefs — beliefs that you get to freely choose.

The story that follows reveals the five inner beliefs held by the world's greatest achievers. These beliefs create the mindset that makes a person unstoppable as they chase their dreams — whatever those dreams may be. For reasons you'll learn in this book, I refer to this unstoppable mindset as "the warrior mindset."

When you think like a warrior, there's nothing that can stop you from achieving your goals.

This story is about a man who has fallen on hard times and can't seem to get back on track. He fears that his best days are behind him and he's desperate to figure out what it is he's doing wrong.

Thanks to some mysterious visits from legendary coaches of the past, the man in this story learns the five inner beliefs that can instantly turn his — or anyone else's — life around.

You may wonder why I chose to use legendary coaches as the mentors in this story and the sports world as the setting.

I did this for the same reason that the field of sports psychology is referred to as "the science of success."

In sports, a successful person's thoughts and actions can be directly evaluated, tested, and confirmed based on their results — results that can't be denied. While the business guru often has an incentive to portray a certain brand image that may not be completely accurate and the self-help guru can be tempted to make promises that are too good to be true, the achiever in sports can't fudge (or inherit) his results. The scoreboard never lies.

That is what makes the sports world the most reliable testing ground for self-improvement principles. The successful leader in sports has proven he or she has what it takes to achieve very difficult goals and their examples show us how to do the same — regardless of our chosen field.

Plus, I personally find a story set in the sports world more entertaining than a story set in an office park.

Though the main character in this story is a college football coach, he's representative of anyone with a big dream and the desire to be successful. The season he endures represents the seasons of life we all must go through when trying to master a new skill, achieve a new goal, or rebound from a setback. Whether you're a coach, athlete, manager, entrepreneur, salesperson, artist, doctor, lawyer, trader, teacher, student, parent, or anyone else striving to move higher in life, you can relate to the main character in this story.

Regardless of the career path each of us may be on, we all experience plenty of unforeseen obstacles as we follow our dreams. The five inner beliefs revealed in this book will empower you to take control of your life and overcome any obstacle that stands in your way.

I hope you'll enjoy the journey as you develop your own warrior mindset.

Darrin Donnelly
SportsForTheSoul.com

"I often refer to our players as elite warriors, not because they are going to war and certainly not because what we are doing is anything remotely as serious as war, but because they are trained in an incredibly rigorous way and are constantly engaged in physical, mental, and spiritual combat."

- URBAN MEYER

1

How did everything that was so good get so bad? Hadn't I already been humbled? Hadn't I already paid for my mistakes? Why were things only getting worse? Were my best days forever behind me? What had I done to deserve this? Why was the world kicking me in the gut when I was already so far down?

Those were the questions running through my mind as I walked up the staircase at two in the morning to share more bad news with Cindy. I knew I couldn't wait until morning. I had to tell her tonight, in case the media already had the story.

I was about to tell my wife that not only was I failing in my career, but now I was also failing in my finances. I had to tell my wife that I couldn't provide for her and our three-year-old daughter.

Cindy usually didn't wake up when I opened our bedroom door this late at night, but she sat up as soon as I walked in.

"Hi, honey," she said with a big smile, more alert than I expected at this hour. "I'm so glad you're home. How was your day?"

I didn't answer. I wanted to, but no words came out. The numbness of despair silenced me.

She turned on the bedside lamp.

"What is it?" she asked.

I sat down next to her, rubbed my eyes, and shook my head.

"You're scaring me." She rubbed my back nervously. "What is it?"

"We're in trouble," I finally forced out. "We're in big trouble."

I felt her stiffen up.

"They fired you?" she asked. "They can't fire you a week before practices start."

"No, they didn't fire me. Not yet, anyway."

How could I tell my wife more bad news after everything she had already endured? How does a man tell the woman he's supposed to protect and provide for that he has failed to live up to all the promises he made her?

I had moved Cindy away from her home state of Oklahoma two years ago to give my dream of being a head football coach one more shot. Being a coach's wife isn't easy, but I assume it's much easier if that coach is a winner. Since taking the job at Wisconsin State, I'd done nothing but lose.

No matter how many games I lost or how upset I was after a game, Cindy had been my constant cheerleader. She kept encouraging me, telling me things would turn around, telling me to be patient, telling me to stick with my vision, telling me to stay positive.

Even through the five-game losing streak we'd endured last fall to finish my second year here with an abysmal 3-9 record, she believed in me. The biggest football fan I knew, Cindy said she just *knew* this team was on the verge of something big.

I wished I had felt the same.

She shrugged off all the newspaper columns and sports radio shows saying I should be fired. She said she couldn't wait for me to prove them all wrong.

But now, after all that, what I was about to tell Cindy would surely crush her. Even the most optimistic person I'd ever known wouldn't be able to deal with this.

"What is it?" she asked again. Fear rising in her voice.

"I'm bankrupt," I said. "*We're* bankrupt."

"What--what are you talking about?"

"Remember those legal issues I told you about a few months ago?" I said. "We couldn't find a way out. I didn't want to say anything until we were certain, but I spent the day dealing with lawyers and accountants. There's no way out. I had to declare personal bankruptcy."

I wanted to break down and cry and tell her how sorry I was for being the failure I'd become, but I couldn't. I was dead inside. I didn't feel anything.

Part of me still didn't believe what was happening.

For the first time in my life, I was surrendering and admitting to myself that I was a failure. I was a defeated man and I didn't know what to do next.

Here I was, a college football coach. A guy who preached responsibility, courage, toughness, and discipline to all the young men I was supposed to be leading. What kind of example had I become?

Cindy sat in silence for what felt like a full minute while I kept my head down. I didn't want to face her.

"My lawyer is fighting with the bank," I said. "He thinks we *might* be able to keep this house for the next six months or so. But he's not sure."

I finally turned to look at her. Tears filled her eyes.

"Say something," I said.

"I'm pregnant," Cindy said.

2

Eight years ago, I was on top of the world.

I remember sitting on the balcony at a luxury hotel in Miami. I had my feet kicked up and the sun in my face on a bright February afternoon, looking out at the Atlantic Ocean while sipping a celebratory cocktail. My agent was nearby on the phone, finalizing the deal that would make me the youngest head coach in NFL history.

At the age of 31, I was about to become a multimillionaire.

I'd spent the last two seasons as an offensive coordinator for the Chicago Bears. We had just gone to the Super Bowl. We lost in a shootout, 51-49, but everyone blamed the defense for the loss. The media agreed that the only reason we had made it as far as we did was because of my offense.

My wide-open, high-octane offense had been called "revolutionary" by the sports media. They called it "basketball on grass." They called me an "offensive genius," "the hottest coach in America," and, "the man with the Midas touch." *Sports Illustrated* put me on the cover of their magazine a week before the Super Bowl with a headline that read: "Chris McNeely's Offense: The Future of Football."

Sitting on that balcony, my agent talked with the Miami Dolphins' upper management team on his cellphone while mine buzzed nonstop. Reporters kept calling or texting to ask me where I was going and if a deal was done. Old friends from back home were offering me their congratulations and asking if the rumors they heard were true.

At least twenty coaches I'd gotten to know over the years also called. They wanted to know if I was assembling a staff yet and whether there would be room for them on it. A few of these coaches were close friends in the business, but my agent told me to not answer a single call. We didn't want any news leaking out and we definitely didn't want to promise anyone a job, he said.

"I respect that some of these coaches are your buddies," he said. "But you'll need to assemble the best staff you can. You're going to be the youngest head coach in NFL history and the last thing you want to do is act like it by hiring a staff of all your old pals."

He made a good point. I didn't argue with him.

"There are going to be a lot of people looking for handouts when this news breaks," he said. "And it's my job to protect you."

I didn't return a single call that day or in the weeks to come. I was just too busy and I didn't want to deal with telling a friend he couldn't be on my staff.

I was so full of swagger. I believed everything the press was saying about me. I really *did* have some kind of mental edge that the rest of the coaching world would never catch up with. It was a gift, I believed. Something that couldn't be explained.

During the press conference introducing me as the new head coach of the Miami Dolphins, I proudly announced that I had a "systematic edge" that would give me an advantage over every other team in this league. I told the media I didn't necessarily need an elite-level quarterback to succeed with my system. It was all about the system, *my* system.

I also told reporters that my goal was not only to win a Super Bowl, but to match Don Shula's legendary 1972 Dolphins team with an undefeated season. I said that was the reason I chose Miami over the other head-coaching offers I had received. I wanted to prove that going undefeated could be done again and I wanted to make sure that Miami remained the only franchise to do it.

Fans were eating up my bold claims and I loved it. While some in the media criticized me for having an out-of-control ego, they couldn't argue with my results.

At least at first.

In my debut season, we stormed out to a 5-0 start. The headlines were already speculating about our potential undefeated run. Everyone around our program was confident that, just as I had declared, we had an inexplicable advantage over everyone else.

I was also enjoying the South Beach lifestyle during this time. Truth be told, that was one of the reasons I chose to accept the Miami job. I was still young and single. I was determined to prove that you could win in this league without sleeping at the office. Especially if you had a "systematic edge" like I did.

After that glorious 5-0 start where we could do no wrong, things started falling apart.

My starting quarterback broke his collarbone in Week 6 and it turned out my backup couldn't be flawlessly plugged into my system the way I had promised at my initial press conference. He struggled to understand my offense and threw seven interceptions in his first three starts. We went 0-3 during that stretch.

Trying to put the brakes on the negative momentum, I made another change at QB. An overtime win the next week put us at 6-3 and I was sure the problem had been fixed. My second-string QB didn't get it, but my third-stringer did.

Or so I thought.

We lost our final seven games of the season to finish 6-10. By the time the season ended, I had started four different QBs.

At the press conference following our final game of the season, I made this regrettable comment: "The offense can't do it all. We need the defense to step up. Coaches, players, everybody. They need to pull their weight."

Looking back, I cringe when I think about saying that.

The media had a field day with me in the offseason. Rightly so.

They said I was too young and immature to be a head coach. They said I was stuck with a coordinator's mindset. They said I didn't understand the concept of team. They said I was throwing my defensive players and coaches under the bus.

In just twelve weeks, I'd gone from the confident genius who was taking the NFL by storm to the immature egomaniac who didn't know how to be a head coach.

I cleaned house in the offseason. I fired all but one of my defensive coaches and three of my offensive coaches. I ripped apart the roster and traded or cut about half the team. I did keep my original starting QB, who would be ready to return from his injury at the start of the new season.

We put together what I thought was a top-notch roster for running my offense and a coaching staff that was one of the highest-paid in the NFL. I couldn't wait to shut my critics up in Year Two.

The comeback season was not to be.

Despite having my original QB back in the lineup, our offense looked awful. No matter what I called, it seemed like the defenses were a step faster in sniffing us out and shutting us down. When I focused on the vertical passing game, we threw too many interceptions. When I focused on shorter, high-percentage passing routes, we couldn't pick up first downs. When I tried to establish a running game, we were stuffed at the line of scrimmage.

Nothing I did worked.

I stopped my South Beach partying and spent every waking hour scouting and scheming. I tried different approaches with the players. I tried the calm, positive-reinforcement approach and I tried the tough-love, negative-reinforcement approach. I ran my staff into the ground with a grueling schedule and extreme demands.

No matter what I tried, none of it worked.

The season was a nightmare. I couldn't stop the bleeding. Three months in, we were 1-11 and the Dolphins fired me.

"You're making a huge mistake," I told the owner. "I'm on the verge of turning this thing around and next year is setting up to be the run we've all been waiting for."

He wasn't buying it. And honestly, neither was I.

Sports Illustrated went from calling me, "the future of football" to declaring me, "the worst coaching hire in modern NFL history."

For the first time in my career, I began to question myself. My "systematic edge" no longer existed. I used to be three or four steps ahead of every defense in the league. Now, it seemed like I was the one always behind and trying to catch up.

Whatever *edge* I thought I had, the football world had caught up with it and shut it down.

To make matters worse, the interim coach who replaced me to finish out the season for the Dolphins won three of his last four games.

After getting fired, I took a year off from the game and focused on business. When it was all said and done, I had still made a few million dollars from my brief stint with the Dolphins. I wanted to "be smart" and put my money to work. I invested in some stocks, three popular Miami-area restaurants, two golf courses, an exciting Silicon Valley startup, and a safe, long-established Texas oil company.

Following my one-year sabbatical, I was itching to get back in the game. My agent made calls about a few vacant head coaching jobs around the league, but he couldn't get me any interviews. He did get me an interview for an offensive coordinator position, but they had zero interest in me and hired someone else.

How had my stature fallen so quickly in this league? The owners and other coaches around the NFL were shunning me.

Rumors were floating around that I had a "toxic personality" and was "difficult to work with." Not exactly a reputation that wins people over, but those personality traits could be forgiven in the world of pro football *if* you knew how to win. The most devastating gossip making the rounds was that I'd "lost my touch" as an offensive coach.

My agent convinced me to eat some humble pie and interview for a college job. After not getting any traction for a head coaching position, we put out some feelers for offensive coordinator spots. I ran into a brick wall with the "Power Five" programs (that is, upper-level teams in one of the Power Five conferences of college football: the ACC, Big Ten, Big XII, Pac-12, or SEC). Apparently, my reputation had trickled down from the NFL and into the premier college jobs as well.

Finally, I landed a few interviews with smaller college programs that were desperate for an offensive jolt and willing to give me a second chance. I was hired as the offensive coordinator at the University of Tulsa, a team with a good football reputation, though one that lacked the huge resources, prestige, and salary offered by a Power Five program. Still, at least I was back in the game.

Making the move to college, especially to one of the non-Power Five programs, was humbling. However, it turned out to be a great thing for my career and my personal life.

Life in Tulsa, Oklahoma, was much quieter than life in South Beach, Florida. This was the type of change I needed. I was able to refocus on the game I loved and I learned the art of recruiting talented young prospects.

During my first year at Tulsa, I met and fell in love with Cindy. She was the younger sister of another coach's wife. We hit it off right away and I knew I had found what I'd been looking for my whole life. I loved her down-to-earth personality. She had a great sense of humor and she *loved* football. We were a perfect fit.

We married the summer after we met. I promised her I would never let her down.

The next summer, we had a daughter and named her Beth.

After three years of running Tulsa's offense, we had a winning team that teetered on the edge of the Top 25 rankings and my offense was ranked in the Top 10 nationally. This brought me renewed attention from the football world.

I was back.

The four years after my stint in Miami had humbled me. I had adapted my offense to the college game and I once again felt like I was a step ahead of defenses. I had learned my lessons and regained my mojo.

Other college programs took notice. I was about to get a second chance at my dream. I was about to prove that I could still be a successful head coach.

At least, that was the plan.

3

I tried to get interviews for a few big-time head coaching vacancies, but they just weren't willing to take the risk on me. A much smaller school, Wisconsin State, offered me the head coaching job.

The Warriors played in the Mid-American Conference, the MAC. Like Tulsa, this school was not at the same level as a Power Five program, but it was still in the Football Bowl Subdivision (FBS) of major college football.

Cindy was nervous about moving so far from her family and the friends she'd grown up with in Oklahoma, but I assured her we'd have bigger and better opportunities in no time. We wouldn't be staying at Wisconsin State long, I promised her.

She said she trusted me and I accepted the job. I signed a three-year contract. Most coaches would never agree to such a short contract, but if things went as I planned, I didn't want a bigger and better school to have to worry about paying some huge buyout to hire me away from Wisconsin State.

Six years after the Dolphins had hired me, I was a head coach again. And this wasn't a rebuilding job like the one I walked into at Miami. I was replacing a coach who was retiring after winning nearly 60 percent of his games during the 15 years he'd spent there. The team he was leaving me had just gone 9-4 and won their second-consecutive bowl game. Those nine wins tied a school record for most wins in a single season at Wisconsin State. Though the program was losing some quality seniors to graduation, a big drop-off wasn't expected.

I was excited about my life again.

We were embraced by the community and Cindy immediately fell in love with the quaint college town. I told her not to get too comfortable with this place. My plan was to take the position at Wisconsin State, modernize their offense, pile up the wins, break some scoring records, and quickly prove to a Power Five school or NFL team that I was ready to return to the big leagues as a head coach. I thought I'd be on to a more prestigious job in two years.

Instead, I damaged my stock as a head coach right away.

During my first year, we finished 5-7. The losing record was Wisconsin State's first in six seasons. We also finished last in the conference in scoring as the transition from a run-based team to a pass-first team didn't go as smoothly as I had hoped. These were not the records I had planned on setting.

The fans and administration remained supportive. They knew I was installing a new offensive system and it would take a little time to recruit the right players.

Things went from bad to worse during my second season. We finished 3-9 and ended the year on a five-game losing streak.

Going into my third season, I was now regretting the fact that I had only signed a three-year contract. There was no question I was on the hot seat and the school could simply let me go after this season if I didn't engineer a huge turnaround.

I was wracked with self-doubt. *Why couldn't I lead this team? Why couldn't I catch a break?*

My life outside of football had turned even worse.

The investments I had made after getting fired from Miami turned out to be anything but "smart." The oil company I bought into fell apart when oil prices collapsed. One of the restaurants I invested in went out of business, another closed up shop after a dispute between the owners, and the third "let me" buy my way out of it for a penalty that cost me about 20 percent of my investment.

But I could've survived those setbacks if it hadn't been for the Silicon Valley startup I'd invested in. The company got sued for millions by another company claiming patent infringement. Our startup lost the case. The way the contract was structured, it turned out I was liable for almost all the debt incurred by this lawsuit because none of the other investors had the liquidity to cover the damages owed. I hadn't legally protected myself. This ruling forced me to sell my stock portfolio and my stake in the two golf courses I'd bought into. This was during a downturn for golf and I only got about half of my original investment back.

Everything that could go wrong *was* going wrong.

When the dust cleared and the lawyers and accountants finished doing all they could to save me, I found out I owed a lot more money than I had to my name and I had no choice but to declare personal bankruptcy.

It was so humiliating.

I couldn't sleep the night I told Cindy I had bankrupted our family and she told me she was pregnant with our second child.

Would we need to move? Would the media pick up this story? Would the players and coaches on my team lose whatever respect they had left for me when they found out about this? How could I focus on the season ahead with all this going on? After all, we were opening up preseason camp in just one week!

Cindy tried to put on a happy face the next day, but I could hear the worry in her voice.

"We just need to trust God that things will work out," she said, though it sounded forced. "I've still got my teaching degree. I'm sure I could get certified in Wisconsin pretty quickly. If nothing else, I'll make a few calls and see if I can get some jobs as a substitute."

"Don't even think about doing that," I said. "You're pregnant and Beth needs you here."

"I could look into daycare."

"We talked about this; you said you love staying home with Beth."

"Situations change, Chris."

I hated myself for putting my family in this situation.

Within two days, the press caught wind of my bankruptcy and a slew of negative columns and talk-show rants followed. This, just days before we kicked off preseason camp.

A scathing column in the local newspaper questioned whether the reason I was losing at Wisconsin State was because I was too focused on my money problems off the field. It said I didn't have the "business sense" to be the "CEO of a football team." It slammed me for being a hothead who made rash decisions and failed to think things through. The column ended with this: "It's time to fire this wildcard coach who serves as an example of how *not* to act for his players and the university. Chris McNeely is simply unfit to be a leader."

On my way into work, I couldn't resist listening to the local sports talk station on the radio. Most coaches will tell you they never listen to these shows, but I think we all tend to fib about that fact.

I heard the show's host, a guy named Randy Tanner and someone I considered a friend, say to his listeners: "The question isn't whether Coach McNeely is on the hot seat. We all know he is and this is the last year of his contract. The question is: is there any way he can turn things around and keep his job at Wisconsin State?"

Randy wasn't saying anything overly-negative about me. I knew what he said was true. But still, I felt like I was eavesdropping on a conversation my friends were having about me. And hearing your friends speculate about whether you should or shouldn't be fired isn't exactly a pleasant experience.

Then came the callers. People called in to slam me for the horrendous job I had done and pile on about my financial problems. They were angry about the state of the program. They couldn't wait for me to get fired.

One caller said: "I'm a Warrior for life, but Wisconsin State should be ashamed of this guy. He can't manage a checkbook, let alone a football team!"

Another called in and said: "Isn't this guy supposed to be some type of offensive guru? That's how he got the job, telling everybody he's a genius, right? Well, if that's the case, then why did we finish last in the conference in scoring each of the last two years? This McNeely guy is a joke and a fraud. He can't be trusted. That's why he's going bankrupt after his shady business deals. If you ask me, it serves him right. We gotta' get him out of here and get him out of here fast."

A similar tone followed with the next caller: "How much of an idiot do you have to be to blow through millions of dollars in such a short amount of time? And he's supposed to be teaching young people how to become adults? What an embarrassment!"

One caller offered a ray of hopefulness, though it wasn't exactly a glowing endorsement for me: "This new junior-college quarterback he's bringing in, Jimmy Baker, he's supposed to be the real deal. I'm anxious to see if he's the type of passer McNeely's been waiting for, so I'll give him at least a few games to see. But, if McNeely can't win with this guy, we've got to fire him before the season is over.

That way, we can get a new coach in here who will get the most out of the new quarterback."

Randy wrapped up the segment this way: "I hear a lot of anger and frustration out there. I share it with you. My feeling is that the only way McNeely remains the coach here is if this team somehow makes it to a bowl game. Based on what I'm hearing from you, it sounds like even a bowl game may not be enough for him to hold onto this job. I would bet that a search for his replacement is already underway. Sorry, Coach."

Randy and his family had been over to my house on a few occasions. We had shared many laughs over burgers and beers following my weekly radio show with him. And here he was, refusing to defend me and glibly chatting with half the state about the fact that everyone wanted me fired. He even went so far as to say he "shared" everybody's anger and frustration.

I knew Randy was just doing his job, but it stung to hear that.

Maybe they were right. Maybe it *was* time for me to be run out of town.

Cindy told me not to listen to the critics and reiterated that she couldn't wait for me to prove them all wrong, but I knew the negative chatter bothered her too. She never stopped encouraging me, though I couldn't help but think she was *forcing* herself to seem optimistic about our future.

Regardless of whether she believed in me or not, I had stopped believing in myself.

Maybe I WASN'T fit to be a leader. Maybe I DIDN'T think things through. How could I get my players to follow me into battle with everyone around our program slamming me and questioning my judgement?

I thought about stepping down and quitting right then. Trying a new career. Accepting the fact that I just wasn't meant to be a head coach.

The night before the start of our preseason camp, I held a meeting with our players and my assistant coaches.

"Tomorrow, our turnaround officially begins," I told them. "I know there's a lot of nastiness being said about me and our program. But just remember, we're all in this together. What they say about me, they're saying about you. Starting tomorrow morning, we all have to do whatever — and I mean *whatever* — it takes to win. From here on out, every single thing you do and every single thing I do must be about one thing and one thing only: winning at all costs."

If the halfhearted response from our players didn't make it clear enough, my defensive coordinator, Chuck DeLuca, made sure I knew how ineffective my speech had been.

Chuck was my right-hand man. I trusted him and appreciated his no-nonsense approach. He was a grizzled 40-year coaching veteran and the main reason I had been able to hire such a well-respected defensive coordinator was because he loved the fishing in Wisconsin. He stopped by my office moments after the meeting.

"You sure that's the approach you want to take?" Chuck asked.

"What do you mean?"

"Some of the things people are saying about you have nothing to do with those kids. They're here to play football, not fight for you in bankruptcy court."

"I was talking about the critics who say *we can't win*," I snapped. "It's got nothing to do with the other crap I'm dealing with, but thanks for bringing it up again."

"It's kind of hard not to, Chris. I had a reporter call me last night and all he wanted to know about was your financial problems and if I thought you could still coach with everything going on."

"And what did you say?" I asked.

"I hung up on him. My point is, it's all everyone is talking about. The coaches are worried about their jobs just like you are and there's some talk about players wanting to transfer. They don't want to go through a coaching change."

"Winning will solve all that."

Chuck didn't respond and I turned my attention to the practice plans on my desk.

I was losing the team and my coaches. Even Chuck, I could feel, had lost confidence in me.

That night, I stayed at the office watching film instead of going home. Every time I saw Cindy and Beth, I got angrier at myself for the position I had put them in. I couldn't face them tonight. I needed to be alone.

When things are going wrong, it feels like there is always *something* more that can be done. As a coach, that means there's always more film to watch or player grades to evaluate or scouting reports to study.

Three hours after midnight, I was having trouble keeping my eyes open.

I turned off the screen I'd been watching and grabbed some extra pillows and a blanket from my closet. I'd be sleeping on my office couch again tonight.

As I tried to fall asleep, thoughts of Cindy sleeping at home alone and Beth playing in her crib flashed through my mind. The images reignited feelings of rage inside me.

Why was this happening?

How could YOU let this happen to me?

I've been humbled, I've learned my lessons. I've already been fired once. Couldn't you make it just a little easier on me this time? It's not just me who is getting hurt; I have a family that is suffering with me. Do you have to kick a man when he's down?!

I realized I was directing these questions at God. This was out of character for me. I hadn't done much praying in recent years. I believed in God and I went to church now and again with Cindy and Beth, but spiritual matters were low on my list of priorities. Now, here I was directing all my anger at a God I didn't think much about.

- *God, if you're there, please help me.*

- *What a joke, if God wanted to help you he wouldn't have let this happen in the first place.*

- *But if you ARE there, please help me.*

- *It's not healthy to blame God or anyone else for your problems. Stop this nonsense and get some rest.*

- *God, I don't know why this is happening, but I need your help. I've tried to do it all on my own and it hasn't worked. If you're there, PLEASE help me. I don't know what to do or where to turn.*

- *Be logical. If God IS in control of such things, he obviously doesn't like you much. Look at what he's doing to you and your family. If he's supposed to be your father, he must be a neglectful one.*

- *God, if you're there please answer me. I have nowhere else to turn.*

This was the conversation taking place in my mind. A back-and-forth debate with myself.

I was getting angrier and angrier. I felt hot and my entire body tensed up. My chest tightened and I heard my heartbeat get louder.

Boom-boom-boom-boom. Then silence.

Boom-boom-boom. Then another pause.

Boom-boom-boom-boom. Silence.

Boom-boom-boom-boom-boom. Another moment of silence.

This pattern continued. Several loud beats, then a pause, then another series of beats.

What is going on? Am I having a heart attack?

I sat up and realized the sound wasn't coming from my heart and the tightness I felt wasn't restricted to my chest. It was a heavy feeling. Like something was weighing down on my head, my neck, my shoulders, *and* my chest. It was the pressure of stress overwhelming me.

Or was it something more?

My forehead was sweaty and I thought I might faint.

Am I having a panic attack?

And WHAT is that sound?

I stood up and realized the sound was coming from somewhere below my office.

I looked out into the hallway and saw that it was empty. The boom-boom-boom-pause continued below and I headed for the stairwell.

As I walked down the steps, the sound got louder.

I came to a door one floor below my office labeled *GYM*. I had worked in this building for two-and-a-half years and I'd never noticed this gym before. Of course, I'd never spent much time in this particular stairwell. The sound was coming from behind that door. As was a rather unpleasant odor.

I pushed open the door and was hit by a smell that reminded me of a locker room that hadn't been cleaned in months, maybe years. What I saw was a basketball court.

The smell made it clear this place was very old, but so did the multipurpose layout. It was obviously being used for other sports besides just basketball. There were only two basketball hoops, one on each end, and there were worn-out wrestling mats in one corner of the gym. At the other corner was a bunch of gymnastics gear, things like padded mats, beams, and trampolines. On the sides of the basketball court were those old-style rollout bleachers instead of fixed seating.

The floor of the basketball court was shiny, like it had been freshly mopped, but the wood surface was stained and chipped throughout.

At one end of the court was a lean man of average height dribbling a worn-out basketball. He was the culprit for the sound I'd been hearing. The boom-boom-boom of his dribble echoed throughout the facility and the pause in the rhythm occurred every time this man shot the ball.

We were the only two people in the gym.

He was wearing what looked like an old track suit. His buttoned-up jacket was blue with yellow trim and there was a round yellow logo with some blue lettering on the left side his chest, but I couldn't see what it said. The man also wore white warm-up pants with blue and yellow stripes down the sides.

He looked like a guy warming up before a game, but he certainly wasn't a current student-athlete. He had to be in his fifties or older. He was wearing black-rimmed glasses and had plenty of gray hair.

"Excuse me," I shouted as I walked his way. "What are you doing here?"

The man picked up his dribble and turned my way. I noticed now that he was wearing a whistle around his neck.

"Shooting around," he shouted back.

Sounds were incredibly amplified in this gym. A gym I never knew existed before this moment.

"Do you realize it's three in the morning?" I asked. "I'm trying to sleep up there." I pointed to the ceiling. "Do you have permission to be in here?"

"I don't need permission," he said. "This is my team's gym."

"Your team? You're a coach here?"

"Yes, I am," he said as he extended his hand to shake mine.

I was now close enough to recognize him. Inside the round yellow logo on his jacket, blue letters spelled out: *UCLA STAFF.*

"I'm John Wooden," he said. "And I'm here to help you."

5

I shook his sturdy hand, but didn't know what to say. This had to be a dream, but it didn't feel like one.

My father had been a high school basketball coach. He had John Wooden's picture on the wall in his office and I'd seen that picture thousands of times. I knew exactly what the legendary coach looked like. This was indeed John Wooden standing in front of me.

"I understand things aren't going the way you hoped," Wooden said.

"Yeah," I said, still confused by what I was seeing. "You could say that."

"I'm sorry to hear that," he said in a grandfatherly tone. "What seems to be the problem?"

"Everything," I said. "We start camp tomorrow. It should be the most optimistic time of the year, but it feels like the start of a slow walk towards my demise."

This was the first time I said out loud what I had been feeling inside for months. There was something about Wooden's genuinely concerned eyes and this surreal setting that made me feel safe about being honest and opening up.

"I just can't stop the bleeding," I continued. "Everyone around here wants me fired. I've bankrupted my family. I can't look my wife and little girl in the eye because of the shame I feel. My wife put her faith in me and I've let her down.

"Instead of optimism, I feel dread about this season. There's a part of me that wants to walk away from it all. Start a new career, I guess, a whole new life."

"You want to quit," he said. It was a statement, not a question.

"I wouldn't put it like that," I said.

"How would you put it?"

"I don't want to quit. I want to *win*. And I want to win now. But I feel like I've lost my edge. I feel like the season has ended before we've even started playing. My players and coaches have lost faith in me. I hate to admit it, but I've lost faith in myself.

"It's like I'm on a sinking ship and there's nothing I can do to keep from drowning."

Wooden listened intently. He put his hand on my shoulder and said, "That's why I'm here."

His reference to *here* snapped me out of my rant.

"Where exactly is *here*?" I asked. "I never knew about a gym down here."

"I brought this place with me," Wooden said. "Everyone calls it the 'B.O. Barn.' Believe it or not, this was the gym we played in when I first arrived at UCLA. We practiced here and even played our home games here, until the crowds got too big."

I looked around at the dingy gym and wondered how a coach could build the foundation for history's greatest college basketball dynasty in a place like this.

I shook my head. "It's amazing you won ten games with a facility like this, let alone ten national championships."

"We upgraded to Pauley Pavilion fifteen years after I arrived at UCLA," he said. "But there's something about this place that still brings back fond memories. Sort of like the old home you miss long after you've upgraded to a much nicer one.

"Though, I will say that I never got used to the smell in here," he said with a smile.

For some inexplicable reason, the fact that I was having a conversation with a man who had been dead for more than five years in a gym that had only existed 2,000 miles away didn't register with me as absurd. My focus was on our conversation. I had a sense that this moment was a turning point for my life. Something told me this man — this

coach, this angel, whoever he was—had t! *s*
needed.

We walked over to the front row of the ro... and sat down. He asked me to tell him everything that had led me to this point of despair and I gave him the entire story of my epic fall from the top of my profession.

When I was finished, he looked at me with caring eyes and said, "I know how you feel."

"Somehow I doubt that," I said. "You were a winning machine. Everybody loved you. You never had to worry about people wanting you fired. You never had to worry about not being able to provide for your family. No offense, Coach, I admire you a great deal, but you had your pick of the best players in the nation and that makes winning quite a bit easier. Here at Wisconsin State, we're stuck with the kids passed over by the bigger schools and have to get lucky with a juco recruit once in a while just to have a chance. I don't think you really understand what I'm going through here."

"I think you have a few facts wrong," he said with a smile.

"First off," he continued, "we missed out on most of the players I recruited. There were higher academic requirements at UCLA and that meant that other schools— schools in our own conference—got the players I could not on due to academics. I'm embarrassed to admit that I complained about those requirements quite a bit during my earlier days at the school. I complained and made excuses just like you're doing right now."

His words cut me, but I didn't argue with him. I *was* complaining and making excuses. I had been for quite some time.

"I can also tell you that people don't remember what a terrible coach I was when I first started out," he said. "I mean, I was just terrible. I began at the high school level. After winning championships as a player in high school and college, I thought I knew everything. I had no patience with the kids. I wanted immediate results. I tried to force them to understand things that came naturally to me as a player. I failed to realize that each person is different and that the same approach won't work for everyone.

"We went 6-11 my first season despite having a much more capable team. This was a very humbling experience because after my playing days, there had been such high expectations for me as a coach. I was falling way short of those expectations.

"My lowest point was when I took my team to a game in my hometown of Martinsville, Indiana. We played against my old high school team and my former coach. This was a team I had been an All-State player with, a team I had gone to three state championships with. I guess you could say I was a star there. Here I was, coming back home to one of the biggest crowds ever in Martinsville to show all my hometown friends, former teammates, and coaches what I had become. They flat-out whipped us. What an embarrassment that game was for me. The long bus ride home was one of the lowest moments of my life.

"After that first season, I wondered if I had what it took to be a successful coach. I know the people who hired me were wondering as well."

"You obviously turned things around after that," I said.

"I did indeed," Wooden said. "I learned some hard lessons quickly and changed my approach. Of course, it took me decades to develop the coaching philosophy that I would become known for.

"People now see me as the coach who won those ten national championships, had the four undefeated teams, had the 88-game winning streak, and coached those All-Americans. They forget what a long and difficult journey it had been before I started seeing those kinds of results.

"Everyone forgets that I spent eleven years coaching high school basketball and seventeen years coaching college basketball before one of my teams finished the season at the top. That's twenty-eight seasons of basketball, nearly three decades of coaching, before we ever won it all."

"I guess I'm one of those people," I admitted. "I didn't realize it took so long for you to start cranking out national titles."

"You also probably didn't realize that I faced bankruptcy. Twice."

The look on my face let Coach Wooden know how surprised I was to hear this.

"It's true," he said. "The first time was as a youngster. The bank took our family farm after a bad vaccination killed our hogs and a drought stunted our crops. My dad — one of the kindest, hardest-working, and most honorable men this world has ever known — never complained. He told me and my brothers: 'Never lie. Never cheat. Never steal. Don't whine. Don't complain. Don't make excuses.' He showed us how to follow those rules by the way he lived his life. Even when our family lost everything, he never cursed, complained, or made excuses. He was the most successful person I ever knew."

Coach Wooden paused to gather himself. Clearly, he was still impressed by the actions of his hero, his father.

"The other time I went broke was right before I got married," Wooden said. "Two days before me and Nell's wedding, to be exact. Through various jobs during college, I had saved up nine hundred dollars. That was a good chunk of dough back then. Today, it would be equal to about fifteen thousand.

"Here I was, excited about my future. I was about to marry my best friend and high school sweetheart. I was so proud that I had been responsible and built up a good nest egg to start the life of our dreams with.

"Then, the bank that held all my savings went bust. I lost everything I'd worked so hard to accumulate. This was *two days* before we got married."

"They just closed up shop without giving you your money back?" I asked.

"They didn't have the money anymore. They lost it. There wasn't insurance on that sort of thing like there is today. Same with Dad's farm. They had no way to protect our family."

I was amazed to hear that John Wooden had shared a financial crisis similar to mine.

"It's not right," I said. "It wasn't your fault or your dad's fault. The people who sold your dad the bad vaccination should've been held responsible. The bank that lost your money should've done whatever they had to do to pay you back. That was *your* money. It's not fair."

"As you know from your own experience, things like this happen. It wasn't your fault that the company you invested in got sued and left you stuck footing the bill."

"That's exactly what is so infuriating." My voice was echoing loudly throughout the gym. "It's not right. It's not *fair!*"

"Things aren't always fair in this world," Coach Wooden said calmly. "Things aren't always going to go your way. That's life. I see so much self-inflicted pain and stress caused by people who think they're entitled to having everything go their way. They think everything should always be fair. But that's not the way this world works.

"It's actually quite liberating when you accept this fact," he added.

"Liberating?" I asked. "It's an awful feeling to accept that. It's a helpless feeling. It means you have no control over anything."

"Quite the contrary," Wooden said. "It means that while you can't control everything, you do have control over the most important things. Therefore, you can stop wasting your time worrying about the things outside of your control.

"How freeing it is to stop stressing over things you can't control. It frees you up to give your full attention to the things you *can* control. And how you handle the things you *can* control determines whether you're successful or not."

Coach Wooden leaned back and let me digest what he was saying.

"Let me ask you something," he said. "I've heard you say you feel like a failure. What would it take for you to feel like a success?"

"That's easy," I said. "Winning. If I start winning games, all my problems will disappear. I'll go from being the broke guy everyone's trying to run out of town to the guy being offered a new contract by this school and probably a number of other schools. As you know, Coach, in this line of work, winning cures everything."

"I thought you might say something like that." The look on Wooden's face told me he didn't approve of my answer.

"You don't agree?" I asked.

"No, I don't," he said matter-of-factly. "Unfortunately, a lot of people would agree with you and I think that's what keeps them from achieving their dreams, whether it be as a coach, as a parent, or as a businessperson."

"You won more national titles than any other coach in history. Obviously, you recognize the importance of winning in this profession. It changes everything. It's what we're all judged on."

Wooden let out a sigh and rubbed his forehead.

"Unfortunately," he said, "you are correct that coaches are judged by the outside world mostly on our win-loss record. The scoreboard matters and we all want to win. It feels awful to lose. I'll concede that.

"The problem, however, occurs with focusing *only* on wins and losses because that's something you can't control."

"Don't tell my boss that," I said with a chuckle. "It's a nice thought, but this isn't pee-wee league. I'm hired to win. And if I don't win enough, I'll get fired. Period."

"That may be, but you've just brought up two things you're focusing on that you don't have total control over: whether you win enough games and whether you get fired. There are many factors outside of your control that determine both of those things. And actually, Chris, your boss could fire you for any number of reasons that don't have anything to do with wins and losses. Coaches with winning records get fired all the time."

"Thanks for reminding me," I said.

Wooden laughed.

"My point is this," he said. "You shouldn't waste time focusing so much of your attention on results because too often you don't have control over those results. And neither do your players."

I shook my head. "But that goes against everything I teach my players. I'm always telling them how they must take total responsibility for their results. They must be held accountable and own their record."

"Then I suggest you change the way you're teaching your players."

"I'm confused," I said. "You're one of the winningest coaches in the history of sports. People have called you the greatest coach *ever*. Are you saying all those wins were just a fluke? A result of lucky breaks that you had no control over? That you never paid attention to the final score?"

"No, not at all," he said. "What I'm saying is that those wins were a result of me and the team's relentless focus on only the things we *did* have control over. Winning was not something I or my players could completely control, so we tried not to focus on it.

"For example, in my eyes, the most successful team I ever coached was the 1962 UCLA squad. Most sports historians wouldn't agree with that statement. The 1962 team is not as famous as many of my other teams. That year, we lost in the Final Four to the eventual champion, Cincinnati. We were undersized and lost by two points in the final seconds. We came within a whisker of being national champions that season. Now, that team was not as talented as many of the UCLA teams I would later coach. But, what I can tell you is that no team I ever coached came closer to achieving their full potential than that 1962 team. Nobody. Not even the undefeated teams that would follow.

"However, despite giving the best effort I've ever seen a team give, the Cincinnati team we faced in the Final Four was better. That loss still stings when I think about it."

"So you admit that you *do* care about winning and losing?" I asked.

"Of course I do. I hated losing. Losing hurts. I'm not suggesting that you pretend that it doesn't or that you naïvely ignore the scoreboard. It's good to set big goals and dream big dreams, like winning a championship. I always *wanted* to win. It feels good to win. I'll never deny that fact.

"But, I tried not to talk about winning and losing with my team. To be honest, I rarely even talked about the opponents we were facing. I did this because I wanted to keep the focus on only what we had total control over. We focused on ourselves, doing what *we* had to do, getting *our* team better. We let other teams worry about us while we only worried about ourselves.

"This is why, despite the fact that my 1962 team lost its final game, I believe they were the most successful team I ever coached. They did the most with what they had. They took what they could control — *their effort* — and gave their very best."

I could now see Coach Wooden's point.

"People often ask me, 'How *did* you win all those national titles, what made the difference?'" Wooden said.

"It's an important question. After all, I didn't run an intricate strategy and nobody would say I was a brilliant play-caller. I stressed conditioning, fundamentals, and teamwork, but lots of other coaches stressed those same things. And it wasn't talent. We had plenty of talented players, but we faced many teams more talented than us."

"If it wasn't your strategy or talent, what was it?" I asked. "Why did you win so many more games than the other coaches you faced?"

"I sincerely believe that the difference was that I didn't talk about winning and losing. I didn't talk about beating opponents. I kept our focus on only what we could control: our *effort* and our *attitude* in the present moment.

"This philosophy came from my Dad. He told me that I should never try to be better than someone else. But, he also said that I should never stop trying to be the very best that *I* could be. 'You have control over that,' he said. 'You don't have control over others.'

"This was the difference-maker. I taught my players that being successful had nothing to with the final score. Success could only be measured by whether you put in the maximum effort. You could lose on the scoreboard and still be successful if you gave your absolute best effort. You could also win on the scoreboard and be unsuccessful if you didn't give your best. Regardless of what the final score says, only *you* can know if you're successful because only *you* can know if you truly did your best.

"By focusing on only the things you can control, it also forces you to think, live, and act in the present moment. This is so important. People waste way too much time and energy thinking about past mistakes or worrying about the future. But there's nothing we can do about the past and the future is determined by what we choose to focus our thoughts and actions on *right now*. You have to focus on the present. That's where your life is lived. How often people forget this."

Wooden's words hit me square. I had been wasting so much time and mental energy stressing myself out by replaying past mistakes or worrying about what might happen in the coming weeks and months.

"Focusing on the present not only means you have to stop *worrying* about the future, but it also means you can't *live* in the future," Wooden said. "You must be fully committed to the task at hand. I understand that from the moment you took this job at Wisconsin State, you already had your eye out for an opportunity down the road, something you think could be bigger and better. How can you give your best here if you've already got one foot out the door?"

I didn't have an answer to Wooden's rhetorical question. He was right. I knew it and he knew it.

"Once my players understood the power of focusing on what they could control right at this very moment, they learned to love the process of giving their best," Wooden said. "They learned to love the process of practicing hard. They learned to love the process of getting better every day. They learned to love the process of putting the team's interests above their own. They learned to love the process of competing with themselves instead of comparing themselves to others.

"It was the *process* we focused on, not the results. Why? Because we have total control over the process. The results, on the other hand, aren't always in our control."

"Sounds a lot like Nick Saban's philosophy," I said. Saban was currently the most successful head coach in college football. I had seen him give a speech at a coaches convention I attended two years prior. During that speech, he constantly stressed what he called "the process."

"It does indeed," Coach Wooden said. "Every coach, leader, teacher, student, entrepreneur, manager, and parent should embrace this philosophy. You can apply it to any area of your life. It works in football just as well as basketball. It works in business just as well as in academics.

It works in parenting just as well as in any other type of leading."

Wooden gave me a smile. He could see that a lightbulb had gone on for me. He knew I was recognizing how wrong my approach had been and what I needed to change.

"And here's the important thing." The coach wasn't finished giving me his keys to success. "When you make a commitment to only focusing on the things you have total control over—the effort you give, the attitude you carry, and the process of improving yourself in the present moment—when you focus on only those things and let the results take care of themselves, it's been my experience that results beyond your wildest dreams tend to follow."

"I can't argue with that," I said. "You won ten national titles in twelve seasons; I think you've proven your philosophy works."

"And I would still believe 100 percent in my philosophy even if we had never won a single championship," he said. "It works. And it works in every area of your life."

Coach then checked his watch.

"It's getting late," he said. "You've got an important day tomorrow and better get some rest."

We stood up and I shook the legend's hand.

"I can't thank you enough for taking the time to help me," I said.

"It's been my pleasure," he said. "Now it's time for you to apply this philosophy to your team and your family.

"Remember, when people get so engrossed in the things they have no control over, it negatively effects the things they *do* have control over. Stop making this mistake in your life and teach your players to avoid this tendency as well. No more obsessing about wins and losses. No more talking about what critics and the media are saying. Focus everything you've got on what you can control: your effort and attitude in the present moment."

I nodded. He had driven home his point and it wasn't hard for me to reflect on my life and see how I was constantly violating this principle. Whether it was my problems on the field or my financial troubles off the field, I'd been spending most of my time worrying about things that were completely out of my control.

"I'll be keeping a close eye on you," Wooden said as he started dribbling the basketball and heading towards the hoop.

"Thanks, Coach." I turned and slowly walked to the gym doors while trying to understand what had just happened.

Was this a dream? What would happen when I left this gym?

Just before I reached the doors, Coach Wooden called out, "And Chris?"

I turned to see Wooden holding the basketball on the far end of the court.

"Success is not something others can give you," Wooden said. "True success can only be attained by knowing you did your very best to become the best you're capable of becoming. That is how I define success. I don't care what the scoreboard says, what your record ends up being at the end of the season, or what your job title is. If you give your best, you will be a success."

And with that, John Wooden turned his attention back to the hoop and put up a beautiful-looking jump shot. *Swish*.

I woke up the next morning with a burst of energy. For the first time in months, I started the day *without* a sense of dread.

I had an intense urge to grab a notebook and start writing. Without thinking and almost as though the words were not my own, I wrote down the following as fast as I could:

I FOCUS ON ONLY THE THINGS I HAVE TOTAL CONTROL OVER: MY EFFORT AND MY ATTITUDE. By focusing on only what I can control, my effort and my attitude in the present moment, I will have the peace of mind that comes from knowing the results will take care of themselves. I will not lose myself in the past or worry about the future. I will focus on the present. If I truly give my maximum effort to be the best that I can be today, I will be successful. NOTHING can take that from me.

As those words fell onto the page, I felt a weight lift off my shoulders. I felt as though I was flushing away all the worries I had been obsessing over.

Would we make it to a bowl game this year? Would my family have to move? Would my new quarterback live up to his potential? Would any of my starters get injured or decide to transfer? Would I be fired? Would I be able to win over all the critics and naysayers who thought I couldn't coach?

These were the questions I'd been agonizing over for the past several months and now I realized that each and every one of them was something I did not have control over. And if I didn't have total control over those questions, then — like Coach Wooden said — I needed to forget about them and focus on only the things I *could* control.

It was freeing to let go of all the worries outside of my immediate control.

I turned my focus to the day ahead, the first day of our preseason camp. I had plenty of things I wanted to get started on and it was exhilarating to let *those* things occupy my mind. I felt the cloud of uncertainty and fear slip away as I started thinking about what I would accomplish on this new day.

At 9 a.m., I met the players and coaches in our locker room. The team was preparing for the first practice of the new season.

I stepped to the front of the room and said, "Men, forget everything I told you last night."

Everyone looked back and forth at each other, stunned and confused. They probably thought I was finally having a mental breakdown.

"In fact," I said. "Let's bury *everything* that has happened to this program over the past two seasons. From this point forward, we're going to do things differently. A lot differently."

Coach DeLuca, my defensive coordinator, gave me a look that asked: *Are you feeling alright?*

"That sign behind me," I said as I pointed to a huge banner I'd hung on our locker-room wall when I first arrived at Wisconsin State. "I need our captains to come up here and tear it down."

The sign read, in huge letters: WINNING IS EVERYTHING.

My captains looked at each other, not sure if this was some kind of test.

"I'm serious," I said, pointing to the four step ladders I'd already placed below the banner. "And don't worry about ripping it. It's time for a change and I want that thing out of this locker room."

They climbed the step ladders and after some initial resistance, the sign tore away from the wall and ripped down the middle. The crumpled and torn banner fell to the floor.

"For the past two seasons, we've been heading down the wrong path," I said. "It's my fault, not yours. I set us down this path by focusing on something we don't have total control over: winning."

Several players shook their heads. Everyone in the room looked at me like I was cracking.

"You don't want us to win?" one of my captains, an all-conference senior linebacker named Braxton Tatum, asked.

"Of course, I *want* us to win," I said. "But wanting and doing are two different things. Our focus needs to be on doing the things that will lead us to winning, not the winning itself. I've had you guys focused on the wrong things, things that you, as individual players, don't always have control over. From this point forward, I want the focus of every man in this room to be on only the things you *can* control: your effort and your attitude in the present moment."

For the next ten minutes, we had a group discussion that sounded an awful lot like the discussion I had with Coach Wooden the night before — in my dream or vision or whatever it was. Slowly, the head shaking turned into nods as we redefined what it means to be successful and went through several examples of the things each player actually has control over versus the things he doesn't.

By the end of our talk, the vibe in the room had changed considerably. There was positive energy rushing through the players and coaches. You could feel it. Everyone was excited to start showing what his best effort looked like.

I finally told the team to take the field and they rushed out of the locker room like it was the opening game.

Coach DeLuca clapped a hand on my back and said with a smile, "Not bad, coach. Not bad at all."

What followed was the most spirited and productive first practice I can ever remember being a part of.

When I got home that evening, I told Cindy things were going to be different. I couldn't explain exactly how, but I was changing my ways.

She let out tears of relief and hugged me tight. I hadn't realized how badly she wanted to see me hopeful again.

The next three weeks of practice flew by as we approached the new season. Braxton, the most vocal leader on our team, was constantly energizing his teammates by shouting out phrases like:

"Maximum effort, baby, maximum effort."

"Nothing but your *absolute* best."

"Effort and attitude, effort and attitude."

These became the battle cries of our preseason camp.

One day after practice, Braxton came up to me and said, "Coach, I'm loving this new approach. Football is fun again!"

I loved hearing that comment, but it also saddened me to think that I had been sucking the fun out of this great game by my past focus on things that were often out of the players' control. If a person is so stressed out about what will happen if the results they achieve aren't satisfactory, they can't let loose and play their best. They tighten up. They get so worried about the things they can't control that they end up making mistakes with the things they do control. It was just like Coach Wooden had said.

This new approach to life also meant more peace at home. You would think someone who had just declared bankruptcy would be stressed to the max, but I told myself that the whole situation was out of my control. It was a bad break and a lesson learned. It was now in my lawyer's hands to see if he could make arrangements for us to keep our home. That was his job, not mine. My job was to get my team ready for the season.

Two days before our season-opener, my lawyer called to tell me he had worked out a deal with the bank. Since my contract with Wisconsin State would either be terminated or renewed based on our performance during the upcoming football season, all parties involved agreed that it only made sense to wait until after the season before foreclosing on our home. At that point, we'd be able to refinance a new mortgage thanks to my new contract or I'd be leaving town anyways.

This was a great relief for Cindy and me. Of course, it also re-emphasized just how much was at stake during the upcoming season.

I won't pretend that worries about things outside of my control didn't keep popping into my mind. But every time they did, I told myself: *I focus on only the things I have total control over.* I would then repeat the words *effort* and *attitude* until the worry subsided.

This technique worked incredibly well. Every time I did it, I felt lighter and more focused. The heavy burden of stress and worry lifted off my shoulders.

7

Our season opener was a nonconference home game against Middle Tennessee. The Blue Raiders were a middle-of-the-road team in Conference-USA (a conference with a stronger reputation than the Mid-American Conference that we played in, but not part of the elite Power Five level of college football). We were seven-point underdogs heading into the game.

It was a gorgeous Saturday afternoon on Labor Day weekend, but our stadium, which could hold up to 30,000 fans, wasn't even half full. Our performance on the field the past two seasons had caused attendance to rapidly decline.

Regardless of the disappointing crowd size, another factor I could not control, our team took to the field full of enthusiasm. We got the ball to start the game and my new quarterback, Jimmy Baker, marched us down the field with a nearly-perfect opening drive. He made great reads and completed seven of his first eight pass attempts, the last one being for a 14-yard touchdown. This was the first time Wisconsin State had led in a game since October of the previous season.

Our defense forced Middle Tennessee to punt on its opening drive. Jimmy looked just as crisp on the second drive as he did during the first. Seven minutes into the game, we had a 14-0 lead.

The rest of the afternoon featured the ups and downs that occur in every football game. We were far from flawless, but we never gave up our lead.

Midway through the fourth quarter, Jimmy threw an interception that was returned 65 yards for a touchdown. We were still leading, 35-31, but the pick six gave Middle Tennessee new life late in the game.

Jimmy threw his helmet down on the sidelines.

"I'm sorry, Coach," he said in anger. "I can't *believe* I didn't see that guy."

In previous seasons, I would have spit out something like, "I can't believe it either," and then lectured and yelled at my quarterback about the importance of taking responsibility and knowing what you're doing late in a game. But I caught myself this time. Why harp on the past, something we had no control over? We can review the play in the film room later and learn from it. Right now, I needed my quarterback focused on what he *could* control.

"What's done is done, Jimmy," I said. "You can't let one play beat you more than once. You're playing a great game out there. Let's focus on finishing it. Focus on the next play."

He nodded.

"Effort and attitude, Jimmy. Effort and attitude. That's all you can control."

I gave him a pat on the shoulder pads and turned back towards the field. My quarterbacks coach looked at me in disbelief. My reaction was the opposite of what he had come to expect from me.

We marched back down the field and finished off the Blue Raiders with a field goal to extend the lead, 38-31.

On the game's last play, Braxton sacked their quarterback with a crushing blow. It was a fitting way to end our losing streak.

As I walked off the field, I looked up to the sky and whispered, "Thanks, Coach Wooden."

Our second game of the season would put Coach Wooden's philosophy to the test. We traveled to East Lansing, Michigan, to face Michigan State in front of 75,000 screaming fans.

The Spartans were ranked number five in the nation. Like most teams in the MAC, our program faced one or two teams from the mighty Big Ten every season. Our conference was considered the Midwest's "kid brothers" to the Big Ten because of how overmatched we were in terms of athletic budgets, facilities, attendance, size, and talent.

The previous season, we had lost to Michigan State 63-12. This year, the outcome was expected to be similar.

On paper, we were facing our toughest opponent of the season and it would take a miracle to pull off an upset. However, there was a part of me that wondered if this new philosophy we were embracing just might make miracles come true. Maybe Coach Wooden would be like an angel on my shoulder and somehow help us pull off the upset of the year.

I envisioned the dramatic headlines that would surely follow our surprising victory. All those critics who wanted to run me out of town would be begging me to stay. We'd get national attention for a win like this. Programs around the country would take notice. Wisconsin State could be offering me a new contract by the end of the week if we were to somehow pull off a win against Michigan State.

As it turned out, during a rainy afternoon in Spartan Stadium, my Wisconsin State Warriors played one of the grittiest games I've ever seen them play. The defense played with a level of physical toughness I didn't know they were capable of. On offense, Jimmy found a way to convert third down after third down to keep our drives alive.

Late in the fourth quarter, we had a shot at knocking off the fifth-ranked team in the country.

With a little over two minutes to play, we were down 28-24. Michigan State had the ball at midfield and faced a third-and-six. We were out of timeouts. If they picked up the first down, they'd be able to run out the clock. If we stopped them short of our 44-yard line, they'd have to punt and we would have one last shot at driving down the field and knocking off the heavily-favored Spartans.

On this crucial play, Michigan State's quarterback dropped back to pass and threw it to his tight end, who was crossing over the middle of the field. He caught it just in front of the first-down line and Braxton was there to meet him with a monstrous hit that stopped the tight end in his tracks. When the referees marked the ball, Michigan State was one yard short of the first down.

The home crowd grumbled in disappointment. Our players hugged each other in jubilation.

But, as our defense was heading off the field, I noticed that the Michigan State offense was staying on the field. Instead of playing it safe and punting the ball away, the Spartans were going to go for it on fourth down and try to seal the game right here.

Without a timeout left, I yelled to our players, "Don't jump offside, be ready for the hard count!"

Coach DeLuca sent out his short-yardage defensive personnel and made his play-call.

The Spartans came to the line of scrimmage and their quarterback barked out the snap count.

"Set...hit. Hit. Hit!"

As I suspected, he was trying to get our guys to jump offside and earn a free first down. Our defense stayed disciplined and didn't budge.

I expected Michigan State to now call a timeout and punt the ball away. Instead, their quarterback looked over our defense, got back under center, and called out an audible. They were going to run a play after all.

After making his adjustments, the quarterback again barked out: "Set...hit."

This time, Braxton, the leader of our defense, went flying upfield and crashed between the center and guard. He was in the backfield before the ball was ever snapped.

He had tried to guess the snap count and he had guessed wrong.

"Offside, defense," the referee said into his microphone as the crowd roared. "Five-yard penalty. First down, Michigan State."

And that was the game. The Spartans ran out the clock and held on for the win.

In the locker room afterwards, Braxton was devastated. Despite playing one of the best games of his career with ten tackles, two sacks, and a pass deflection, he blamed himself for the loss.

"I don't care what that scoreboard says," I told the team. "What I saw out there today was the single best effort I've ever seen a team give. And that especially includes the performance I saw from the best linebacker and leader a team could ever ask for: Braxton Tatum."

The team clapped its approval and tried to console each other, especially Braxton.

It was painful. Losing hurts. No matter how hard you try or how close you come.

"I know it doesn't feel like it, but you are *all* winners today," I said. "I'm proud of you and I want you to be proud of yourselves."

Though I'd never been a believer in so-called "moral victories" prior to my chat with Coach Wooden, I now believed exactly what I told the team. Their performance really was something to be proud of. If we're judging ourselves on only what we can control — our effort and our attitude — then we had been successful. We just happened to be facing a much more talented team on this particular Saturday.

When we arrived back at the Wisconsin State campus, a few dozen of our fans were there to greet us and show their support, which was touching.

That night I told Cindy, "I feel like I passed a crucial test today."

"How so?" she asked.

"It's easy to stick with a new philosophy when things are going your way. It's easy to say you're not going to focus on results when you *win* and achieve the results you want. The test comes when you lose. Can you still feel good about your approach? Are you committed to it?

"I can say with certainty that I am *all in* on this."

Little did I know that a much bigger test would come the following week.

9

Despite the heartbreaking loss to Michigan State, there was a positive vibe on campus the next week.

During my weekly radio show with Randy Tanner, several fans called in to say how excited they were about Wisconsin State football once again. One fan called in to apologize for "misjudging" me. He said he was now fully behind me. I laughed and said that while the season was still young, I did feel good about the direction we were heading. I also wondered if he was one of those callers I'd heard just a few weeks before calling me a fraud and an embarrassment to the university.

After the 1-1 start to the season, our next opponent was the Iowa Tech Bearcats. This was an FCS-division school, which meant it was classified as a division below the FBS division we were members of. FCS schools were smaller, had fewer scholarships to offer athletes, lower athletic budgets, etc. On top of that, Iowa Tech was 0-2 heading into our game. We were expected to *easily* beat this team.

Though our players were disappointed after the close loss to Michigan State, we bounced back and had a good week of practice. The other coaches and I were excited about the way we were playing.

In particular, I was very impressed with Jimmy, our new quarterback. He had picked up the offense better than I expected and he had a more accurate arm than I had realized when scouting him. We may have lucked out by catching a junior-college prospect who was overlooked by the Power Five schools.

Jimmy was also embracing our new team philosophy of focusing on only what we could control. He played loose, but focused on the present. When he made mistakes, he was learning to bounce back quickly.

Despite facing what was considered a weaker opponent in Week Three, our home crowd was much better than the one we played in front of to open the season. The fans were starting to believe we had something special going on here and they wanted to be a part of it.

We got off to another fast start against Iowa Tech. We built a 14-0 lead on our first two drives and then saw their starting quarterback leave the game with an injury. The backup quarterback was a freshman who didn't look prepared for the opportunity. He threw an interception on his first pass attempt. That set up another quick touchdown for us and we were up 21-0 at the end of the first quarter.

I noticed an ugly vibe on the Iowa Tech sidelines. Their head coach was screaming at his players and his assistants. The assistants were screaming just as hard at the players they were coaching. I saw a lot of yelling and shoving between the players as well. A lot of blaming and complaining. I wondered if my sidelines used to look like that.

With a 31-3 lead at halftime, I told our second-team players to be ready for some playing time in the second half.

Unfortunately, the momentum quickly shifted against us and our second-team squads never got the chance to enter the game.

Iowa Tech drove down the field and scored a touchdown on their opening drive of the third quarter. This cut our lead to 31-10. We answered with a long drive of our own, but fumbled the ball away inside their 10-yard line.

"C'mon, guys," I said as the offense jogged back to our sidelines. "What happened to giving maximum effort? We've got to stay focused."

Another long drive followed, but we held the Bearcats to a field goal. Leading 31-13 at the start of the fourth quarter, Jimmy threw a wild pass that was intercepted. I couldn't believe it.

"If we're not careful, we're going to lose this game," I said to no one in particular on the sidelines.

On their next drive, the Bearcats converted on three fourth downs, capped off with a trick-play touchdown to cut into our lead. We were up 31-20 with six minutes left in the game.

On the ensuing kickoff, our return man fumbled the ball into a pile of bodies. When the referee cleared out the pile, he signaled it was Iowa Tech's ball. A short drive later, they scored another touchdown.

The Iowa Tech players went nuts. Our players stood in shocked silence. We did stop their two-point conversion attempt, but the score was now 31-26 with two-and-a-half minutes left to play.

They attempted an onside kick, but we recovered it. I let out a sigh of relief and heard Iowa Tech's head coach screaming at his kicker, "That was awful! Absolutely awful! That's why you'll never earn a scholarship here!"

I shook my head in disgust.

All we needed was a first down to put this game away and survive the scare from a lower-division school.

I stopped Jimmy on his way onto the field and said sternly, "Play smart. Whatever you do, *don't fumble the football.*"

He gave me a nervous nod. Two plays later, Jimmy fumbled the snap and Iowa Tech took over with 45 seconds left.

It was like a bad dream.

Iowa Tech's freshman quarterback, a kid who looked completely lost when he first entered the game, now decided to drive his team down the field as if he was the second coming of Joe Montana. He hit each of his passes perfectly and managed the clock like an all-pro. With three seconds left, at the 15-yard line, this undersized kid took the snap, scrambled around, somehow slipped away from three of our defenders who had a shot at sacking him, and threw a prayer into the back corner of the end zone. The ball landed perfectly in the hands of an Iowa Tech receiver. I saw the referee signal touchdown and I felt like somebody had just punched me in the gut.

Final score: Iowa Tech 32, Wisconsin State 31.

In the most humiliating performance of my coaching career, we let a 31-3 halftime lead slip away and turn into a loss.

I stormed my way to the locker room, rage rushing through my veins.

Chuck stopped me on the way in.

"Coach, I think you should take a minute before you address the team," Chuck said.

I brushed his hand away.

"This was the single worst performance I've ever seen from a football team," I told my players. "What I saw out there today was a group of quitters. You all quit in that second half. You quit on me, you quit on this university, you quit on each other, and you quit on yourselves. You should all be ashamed. In my entire life, I've never been more disappointed in a team."

Just about every player in the room had his head down. Some cried. Some shook their heads.

"As you guys know, we have a bye week next week," I said. "I told you you'd have a few days off. Well, forget that. I want everyone ready to practice on Monday. And when we start practicing, you're in for a rude awakening. If you're not going to give me all you've got in a game, I'm going to work it out of you in practice. Get ready for hell, gentlemen."

I wanted to punish them for the loss. I was so enraged with their ugly second-half performance. All I could think of was working them into the ground.

Somewhere, Coach Wooden must have been shaking his head in disappointment.

10

Watching film of the game only made me angrier and by the time we started practice again on Monday (a practice we weren't originally planning on having), I wasn't feeling any sympathy towards my players. True to my word, we ran one of the most exhausting practices I've ever conducted.

"Coach, maybe it's time we time we call it a day," Chuck said to me after two-and-a-half grueling hours. "The kids can barely hold their heads up and I don't want anyone getting hurt."

"You saw what happened in the fourth quarter on Saturday," I said. "They need to learn what it means to leave it all out on the field."

I had the team line up for our "two-minute drill." This was essentially a scrimmage where the first-team offense would drive down the field against the first-team defense as though the game was on the line. Normally, this drill wasn't full-contact, but I wanted to see who had the guts to prove themselves. I told the team this was a "live" drill.

"Play to the whistle and no pulling back," I told them. "Give it everything you've got. I want to see some big hits."

Unfortunately, they did exactly what I asked.

Three different players left the field with injuries during the drill. On the final play, Jimmy took off scrambling towards the endzone and dove for the goal line. Braxton crashed into him with a thunderous hit. Since this was an unplanned scrimmage, we didn't have refs and it was too close to tell whether Jimmy scored or not. The two squads argued, pushed each other, and then erupted into an all-out brawl.

It took us close to five minutes to break it up. Even some of the coaches got into it with each other. When the dust cleared, two players had broken hands, one guy had a broken jaw, and my starting quarterback couldn't move his throwing arm.

Jimmy had been at the bottom of the pile and it was never clear whether he hurt his shoulder on the dive to the endzone or in the fight afterwards. All we knew is that he now had to go in for x-rays.

What had I done?

Not only had I turned my team against each other, but I had also injured my starting quarterback and several other key players. All the positive energy we had built up during preseason camp had been flushed away. There was now hatred and bitterness burning through our team. Everyone, including me, wanted to get as far away from each other — and the game of football — as we could.

Later that evening, the team doctors told us Jimmy's shoulder wasn't dislocated, but it was badly strained and he would need to miss two to three weeks to rest it.

After a tense post-practice coaches meetings and some unproductive film study, I knew I needed to cool off before going home. I was so angry. Angry at myself, angry at my team, angry at the game I used to love. I was angry at everything.

With a record of 1-2, I could feel the season slipping away. I wondered if Coach Wooden had ever lost his passion for basketball. I had certainly lost mine for football.

I figured I could use a drink to calm my nerves before I went home, but I didn't want to stop at a busy bar or restaurant where I'd be recognized.

I turned down some quiet side streets looking for a hole-in-the-wall type of place.

On 18th Street, several blocks from the main hub of college bars at the center of this town, I noticed a brick building with blue awnings over the windows and a lit up blue neon sign hanging on the corner. The sign read, "THE BLUE ROOM," and had a piano image at the bottom.

A smaller sign above the door declared, "Live Jazz Tonight." A small, out-of-the-way joint with music that would be loud enough to drown out my thoughts and keep people from bothering me. Exactly what I was looking for on this night.

As I entered the Blue Room, the jazz band on stage finished their song and I felt like the fifty or so patrons all turned my way. I'm not sure what made me stand out more, the fact that my Wisconsin State windbreaker and hat highlighted that I was the only person not wearing a snazzy suit or the fact that I was the only white person in the room.

After some brief—and a few unwelcoming—glances my way, everybody went back to what they were doing. I headed straight for the bar.

"Coach McNeely, I've been waiting for you," someone shouted from off to my right.

I turned to see an older man in a midnight blue pinstripe suit. He was sitting alone and smiling. He motioned for me to have a seat at his table. I assumed he was a fan who recognized me and was now trying to make a joke about how he'd been waiting to give me a piece of his mind.

"Do I know you?" I asked, as I walked over to his table and the band on stage started into their next song.

"I don't think we've formally met before, if that's what you mean," the man said, still smiling.

He had a head of white hair, he dressed sharp, and he looked athletic. I would've guessed he was in his fifties or sixties. He had a vibe of being someone important, like he might be the owner of the place.

"You look like you could use a drink," he said.

I nodded and sat down. He motioned for a waitress who promptly walked over to our table.

This man gave off an overwhelmingly positive aura. It was hard to describe. He was energetic and confident. One of those guys who lit up a room. At the same time, he didn't come across as bombastic or egotistical, as people like that sometimes can. He put me at ease. He made me feel...happy.

"What can I get you?" the waitress asked.

"I guess I'll have what he's having," I said, pointing to the man's drink, which looked like clear gin with a lime slice.

"Better make it a double for my friend," the man said with a big smile.

The waitress looked confused. "Uh, sure thing," she said, before heading back to the bar.

"Chris McNeely," I said as I reached out to shake the man's hand.

"I know who you are," he said. "I'm Buck O'Neil." He shook my hand while tapping the table to the beat of the music with his other hand.

The band on stage was good. You could tell these guys were jazz pros. The music was loud, but we were far enough from the stage that we could still talk comfortably.

"Why do you look so familiar to me, Buck?" I asked.

"I used to be a ballplayer, but that was before your time. After that, I was a coach like you. Baseball was my sport. I did a lot of interviews about the sport later in my life, that might be where you've seen me."

"No kidding?" I said. "Did you coach here, at Wisconsin State?"

He laughed and shook his head. "No, man, I coached pro ball. Back when I was coaching, there's no way a guy like me could've coached here."

"You coached a pro team?" I was genuinely impressed. "Where at?"

"I was a player and manager for the Kansas City Monarchs," he said.

The waitress arrived with my drink.

"I'm not familiar with them. Is that a Triple-A team?" I asked Buck. I noticed the waitress roll her eyes as she left.

Buck laughed hard. "No, no, man. We were big-time. Some say we had the best team in all of baseball when I was playing there. We won pennants left and right. It was a magical run."

"Uh-huh," I said skeptically. I was starting to wonder if this guy had had a few too many cocktails. "Then how come I've never heard of them?"

"Maybe because you don't know much about baseball," he said.

"Maybe that's true," I said, trying to be polite.

"How can you not know about the Monarchs? Maybe you've heard of some of their players. Ever heard of Satchel Paige? How about Ernie Banks? How about a guy named Jackie Robinson?"

"Of course, I've heard of them. But I know Jackie Robinson played for the Dodgers and Ernie Banks played for the Cubs."

"That's true, and Satchel played with the Cleveland Indians. Actually, Satchel also played a game with the Kansas City A's, back in 1965. He was 59 years old and became the oldest player ever to play in the majors. He pitched three shutout innings that day and gave up just one hit. I've got *a lot* of Satchel Paige stories, but I don't want to get off track. The point is, before any of those players were allowed in the majors, they played for the Kansas City Monarchs. We were the New York Yankees of the Negro Leagues. In fact, I'm pretty certain our 1942 team would've regularly beaten the Yankees if we'd been given the chance to play them."

This guy seemed to believe what he was saying, but the time period he was referring to was way too long ago to be plausible.

"You want me to believe that you played baseball on a team in the 1940s?" I asked.

"Sure did. After my playing days with the Monarchs, they made me a player-manager. Whether I was playing or managing, though, we kept winning championships. It was a dynasty, man.

"After the color barrier was lifted and the Negro Leagues ended, I became a scout for the Chicago Cubs. One year, they made me a coach, which made me the first black coach in the history of Major League Baseball. They never let me coach on the field, weren't ready for that, but it was still a good time. After that, I went back to being a scout, which I loved.

"I spent 32 years with the Cubs and decided to retire. But then, the Kansas City Royals hired me to be a scout for them. I was 77 years old when the Royals hired me. All my life's been about baseball. Either coaching or playing. I can't imagine a better way to make a living."

Buck spoke with such conviction, but some quick math told me that if he was who he said he was, he'd have to be at least 100 years old. Impossible, considering how young he still looked.

Unless...

I leaned in close to him, looked both ways over my shoulder to make sure I wasn't overheard, and said, "Buck, did John Wooden send you to see me?"

11

Buck laughed again. Whatever he was drinking sure did make him happy.

I took a sip of my drink and tasted...nothing. It was water, with a hint of the lime slice that was dropped in it.

"I think the waitress accidentally brought me a water," I said.

"You asked for what I was drinking." Buck said. "That's what I'm drinking."

I glanced around the place again and noticed that while everyone was looking spiffed-up in their suits, the style was more 1940s than 2010s.

"Is this a dream?" I asked.

"Might as well be," Buck said. "Jazz makes any night a dream come true. Jazz and baseball. Two of the greatest inventions known to man."

I took another drink of water, wanting to be certain it wasn't something more potent.

"How did you know I'd be here?" I asked.

"Someone mentioned you'd be stopping by," Buck said. "I've been dead almost ten years and I've found that a lot of people seem to stumble into this place at just the right time in their lives. I don't know how it happens. It just does."

"Did Coach Wooden tell you to talk to me?"

"Believe it or not, I answer to a higher power than Coach Wooden. Even if the man did win ten national titles." Buck laughed again.

"Why are you here?" I asked, getting more confused by the second. I couldn't be dreaming again. I had *driven* to this place.

"I think the question you should be more concerned with is, 'Why are *you* here?' You've got a serious problem right now and somebody thinks I can help you with it."

Buck was looking at me more seriously now.

"What exactly do you think that problem is?" I asked.

"You don't look happy, man," Buck said. "In fact, you look miserable and bitter."

"Why don't you tell me what you really think?" I said with a forced chuckle.

"Why don't you tell me what it is you're so upset about?"

"Maybe it's because this afternoon I witnessed what was by far the single worst practice I've ever seen in my life. It ended with a bench-clearing brawl and an injury to my starting quarterback. Oh, and this is just two days after I saw my team go out and give one of the worst second-half performances in the history of college football.

"I think I'm justified in being a little ticked off at the moment."

"You sure about that?" Buck asked. "You sure your unhappiness is justified by your problems and not the *cause* of them?

"Let me ask you another question," Buck said, before I could answer. "What do you have to be so bitter about?"

I gave him a look that asked, *are you kidding me*?

"And don't give me all that crap about your time at Miami, your losing season last year, your bad investments, I already know all about that stuff," Buck said. "Everybody has to deal with things like that. I want to know why you think you're entitled to be so upset and bitter about it."

I wasn't sure how to respond.

"Let me tell you something," Buck jumped in. "My grandfather was kidnapped as a little boy and brought to America on a slave ship. He used to tell me stories about his time as a slave, working for a slave owner on a plantation in the Carolinas. Can you imagine growing up like that? But he also told me he wasn't bitter. He was an optimist and he lived to be 98. He used to tell me black people could achieve any dream if they worked hard enough for it. He told me this during a time when Jim Crow was very much alive and segregation was the norm. He said he thought there was enough good in any white man to eventually overcome racism. Can you believe that? If anyone was entitled to holding onto bitterness, it had to be a former slave, right?"

"Most definitely," I said, shaking my head at the thought of how cruel humanity could be.

"I grew up in the segregated South," Buck said. "And back then, whenever the roads needed work done, the county would round up a bunch of young black men, charge them with vagrancy, and put them on chain gangs for a few months, until the road work was done. And black people weren't allowed to attend our town's high school. It was for white kids only. We couldn't go to school after the eighth grade. My point is, black people weren't treated fairly. But my mother didn't let that stop her from wanting something better. She started her own restaurant and encouraged us to dream big dreams and live them out.

"My dream was baseball. I knew I'd never be allowed to play in the majors, but thanks to a guy named Rube Foster starting the Negro National League, there *was* an opportunity for blacks to play professional baseball. In fact, Rube showed me that there was a way for a guy like me to make a *living* in baseball. I was 12 years old when I realized that was what I wanted to do. My dream was to be a ballplayer and then a coach after that.

"Was my dream easy? Of course not. In the early days, I can remember going on long road trips across the country with teammates, looking for any tournament we could play in. Most hotels wouldn't allow blacks to stay there and most restaurants wouldn't allow us to eat there, so we'd sleep wherever we could and eat whatever food we could find. We'd sometimes sleep outside in hobo camps and sometimes the only thing we could find to eat was stale bread. But you know what? It was better than working on a celery farm."

"A celery farm?" I asked.

"That's where I worked when I was a kid. It was hard, hot, brutal work. I can remember one day saying, 'Damn, there's got to be something better than this.' My father, who also worked on the celery farm, heard me say that. I'll never forget what he told me later that night. He said, 'There *is* something better than this. But you can't find it here. You're going to have to go out and get it.'

"When my dad said that to me, it was a turning point in my life. He made me realize that the world wasn't going to hand me the life I wanted to live. I had to *decide* what I wanted out of life and then go get it myself!

"For me, I wanted to live a life in baseball. I *loved* baseball. I decided then that I was going to go out and *make* a life in baseball."

Buck then told me about his amazing journey through life. He told me how he worked his way onto the legendary Kansas City Monarchs team. He shared stories about Satchel Paige. He told me about future Hall-of-Famers like Josh Gibson, Cool Papa Bell, Oscar Charleston, Roy Campanella, Ernie Banks, and Jackie Robinson; these were all players who got their start in the Negro Leagues because they weren't allowed to play in the majors. He rattled off dozens of names of black players who never got the opportunities or the attention they deserved.

He told me more about what life was like playing in the Negro Leagues. The good and the bad. The good, like how he and his Monarchs teammates were treated like celebrities in downtown Kansas City during the 1930s and 1940s. And the bad, like when the players weren't allowed to eat or use restrooms at road stops all across America. The good, like how 50,000 fans would show up in Chicago to see the annual Negro League's all-star game. And the bad, like the ugly name-calling they endured and some unforgettable run-ins with the Ku Klux Klan.

It was fascinating to hear Buck talk about how they used to play in barnstorming tours in the offseason, where a team of black all-stars would play against a team of white all-stars made up of baseball's most famous players — guys like Stan Musial, Bob Feller, Lou Gehrig, and Ralph Kiner. He told me how the black teams had a winning record in those games, further making the case that many of the best baseball players in America at that time played in the Negro Leagues and never got the chance to play in the majors.

"Makes you wonder, what if baseball hadn't been segregated?" I said. "What if all those guys would've gotten a shot at the majors? How much more money you guys would've made. How much easier life would've been for you."

"Yeah," Buck said, "But we were playing baseball. And that's my point. Despite all those disadvantages, all those things we could've complained about and gotten bitter over, we were living our dreams. From time to time, we'd all talk about how we wished we could get a shot in the majors, but at the end of the day we were playing the game we loved. We *loved* what we were doing!"

Buck looked off with a smile as he reminisced about the game he had so much passion for.

"Now, my question to you is this," Buck said. "Are you doing what you want to be doing with *your* life? Are you doing what *you* love?"

I thought about it for a moment and he waited. He wasn't going to let me off the hook. He wanted an answer.

"I do love the game of football," I finally said. "At least, I think I do. There was a time when I was certain I did, but these last couple years have worn me down. I've been questioning if this is still the right career for me."

"And why is that?" Buck asked. "Is there something you'd rather be doing with your life? Because let me tell you, nobody's forcing you to be a football coach."

"I've wanted to be a head football coach for as long as I can remember, Buck. I don't know what's happened to me. I'm wondering if I have what it takes to make it in this business. The losing. The critics. My own self-doubt. It's all taken the joy out of the game for me."

"No, no, no," Buck said. "You've got it all wrong. You can't blame anything *outside* of you for taking away your joy. Only you can take the joy out of your life.

"I told you about all the unfair things I went through, but I didn't let those things rob me of my joy and my love for the game of baseball. If my grandfather could stay optimistic after everything he went through, what excuse do any of us have? No, man, you've got to stop letting stuff *out there* take the joy out of your life. Passion and optimism, these are things you have to give yourself. Nobody can give them to you."

"I hear what you're saying, but I can't ignore reality," I said. "There is a lot of negative stuff going on right now in my career and in my life. I can't ignore those things."

"There's a big difference between ignoring those things and dwelling on them," Buck said. "Sure, there's negative stuff out there, always will be. But you've got to zap those negative thoughts and focus on the positive. You've got to keep your focus on the love of the game and the good things in your life. You've got to take the time to be thankful for all the wonderful things you have going for you.

"Finding what you love to do is the first step. After that, you have to remind yourself every day why you love it. Otherwise, the world can strip away your passion.

"The world isn't fair and it isn't easy. You know this. But you have so much to be thankful for. You have so much going for you. Start counting your blessings and you'll quickly realize they're trouncing your curses.

"You have a job that tens of thousands of people would love to have. You make your living in a sport that millions of people love. You're surrounded by a loving family and friends that care about you. You've got to remind yourself of these things."

"It's true," I said. "I do have a lot to be thankful for."

"Damn right, you do," Buck said. "You can't let negative *outside* forces take away the passion and joy from *inside* you. That's what makes a man bitter. You focus so much on all the negatives that you forget to focus on all the positives you have going for you. Like a job you're so lucky to have!

"Let me tell you this, I believe there is an opportunity buried within every obstacle. Most people see a negative situation and write it off as another reason not to keep moving forward, but happy and successful people find the *opportunity* in that situation.

"When I was a scout for the Cubs, for a long time I was one of the only black scouts in all of Major League Baseball. A lot of people would see this as a negative, a disadvantage, another unjust situation where the odds were stacked against me because I was excluded by the rest of the scouts and left out of the network of connections they had with each other. I chose not to see it this way. In fact, I saw me being one of the only black scouts as a huge *advantage* for me.

"When I scouted black players on black teams, I could blend in with the crowd. Whereas when a white scout was on hand, everybody knew he must be a scout from the majors. And players played differently when they knew scouts were watching.

"I also had a big advantage when meeting with the prospect's family. If several scouts were after a hot black prospect, who do you think the parents would want their son to head off to the big city with? One of the many white scouts trying to sign the kid or me, the only black scout who took the time to go to church with them and have dinner with them?

"If you love what you do, you find a way to turn every obstacle into an opportunity.

"But it all starts with loving what you do. You have to love what you do. That's the only way to live your life. I don't care what your job is, whether it's prestigious or makes you a lot of money or any of that other stuff. You've got to *love* what you do!

"Here's another reason why doing what you love is so important: if you don't love what you do, you're going to get beat by somebody who does!

"You've got to take pride in your vocation and find the joy in it every day. That doesn't mean you have to be smiling ear-to-ear throughout the day. You can be intense and focused and still be living with joy and passion. The important thing is that you live the life you were born to live.

"And if you don't love your job or if it makes you miserable, then you need to go do something else with your life."

Seeing it this way — realizing that I could go do a number of other things with my life if I wanted to — made me recognize that I did have the job I had always dreamed of having. I was the head coach of a football team. There wasn't anything I'd rather be doing with my life.

What *did* I have to complain about? Why *was* I letting outside critics ruin the fun of this game for me? I *loved* this game. I *loved* this job. I was letting stress, worry, and bitterness drown out the passion I'd had for the game. A passion I'd had ever since I was a little kid.

"Let me tell you about a Hall-of-Famer I once coached," Buck said. "Ernie Banks would eventually be known as 'Mister Cub' because of how much joy he brought to Chicago fans. But he wasn't always the joyful player everyone remembers.

"In 1950, I was manager of the Monarchs and we signed Ernie. He was a 19-year-old kid from Texas who was extremely shy. He played tight and kept everything inside.

"I told him, 'Be alive, man! You gotta *love* this game to play it.'

"Eventually, Ernie embraced what I was preaching. People now remember him for the joy and enthusiasm he played the game with. He had a long career and a long life after baseball.

"Ernie tells people that he learned to play the game that way from me, which is nice of him to say, but what I was telling him is what I told all my players. And it's what I'm telling you. It's something I think is true for everybody. *You have to love what you do!*"

Buck lived this truth and his joy was infectious.

It was then that the waitress startled me out of our conversation.

"Are you two about ready to wrap this up?" she asked.

I looked around and realized that Buck and I were the last patrons left in the Blue Room. The band had finished their set and the bartenders and waitresses were cleaning off the tables. I had lost myself in our conversation. I looked at my watch and saw that it was nearly three hours past midnight.

We wrapped things up and I thanked Buck for making me realize the importance of reigniting my passion and being thankful for the opportunities I had.

He was right. *I* was responsible for letting the negative outside forces steal my inner passion and joy. *I* was the one letting self-doubt and worry into my life. *I* was the one who had let bitterness creep into my mindset.

As we were leaving, I had one more question for Buck.

"Despite the fact that you lived your life doing what you love, isn't there a part of you that is just a little bitter that you played in an era of segregation and so much injustice? Had you been born just a decade or two later, you could've had a long career in the majors and you probably would've ended up managing a Major League team."

Buck shook his head.

"What good does bitterness ever do anyone?" he asked. "Hatred does nothing but harden your heart. It only hurts you. I'd rather live by love. Loving others and loving what you do. That's the only way worth living."

"I thought you would say that," I said with a smile.

"My friend Satchel Paige once said, 'Never let your head hang down. Never give up and sit down and grieve. Find another way. And don't pray when it rains if you don't pray when the sun shines.' That's a pretty good way to live your life, if you ask me."

I nodded.

"Don't shed any tears for me," Buck said. "I lived my life to the fullest. I did what I loved and I spread love to everyone I could. I don't regret when or where I was born. Had I been born at another time or place, I'm sure there would've been plenty of other things I could've found to complain about. No, I was right on time, man. I took my best shot at life and that's all anyone can do."

"Sounds like something Coach Wooden would say."

"Yes, it does," Buck said with a big laugh. "Yes, it does!"

12

Just as I had after my experience with John Wooden, the morning after my meeting with Buck O'Neil I had an overpowering urge to grab a pen and start writing. Again, the words didn't feel like my own. As I wrote, I heard Buck O'Neil's voice. Here are the words that landed on the page:

I LOVE WHAT I DO AND I ATTACK EACH DAY WITH JOY AND ENTHUSIASM. I am passionate about what I do for a living. I'm grateful for the talents and interests I've been uniquely blessed with; they lead me to my purpose in life. I am fully committed to doing something I love and something I was born to do. I do not wait for someone to hand me the life I want to live, I go out and create it on my own. My passion for what I do gives me a competitive advantage over those who don't have the same level of passion. I zap negative thoughts and focus on the positive. I find opportunities in every obstacle. Life is good. I am grateful for all the wonderful blessings in my life.

The words put a smile on my face.

"Good morning, ladies," I said cheerfully to Cindy and Beth at the kitchen table that morning. "How's everybody doing today?"

Cindy got up from her breakfast, walked over to me, and gave me a hug.

"I'm so glad to see you smiling," she said. "You have no idea how much that affects me."

It's easy to forget what an impact our own attitude has on those around us. Attitudes are contagious. Not only do we owe it to ourselves to be positive, but we owe it to those we love.

On my way to campus that morning, I took a turn down 18th Street. The Blue Room I had visited the night before was not there.

This didn't surprise me as much as it *saddened* me. Buck may have been the most joyful, full-of-life person I ever met. It made me sad to think I might never get to talk with him again.

Once I got to my office, I called in all the coaches and took responsibility for the disaster that was Monday's practice. When a leader makes a mistake, he must own it. My staff seemed to appreciate the gesture. I also told them we needed to shift gears and bring the players back together. We traded ideas and came up with a plan.

That afternoon, as the players prepared for practice, still looking exhausted and miserable, I burst into the locker room.

"New plan, men," I said. "Take off your pads. We're going to the movies today."

First they looked stunned. Then I saw some smiles. Next thing you know, this locker room full of highly-trained, muscle-bound football players who had tried to destroy each other the day before erupted into glee. They looked like a classroom of third-graders who had just been told school was cancelled, high-fiving and laughing with each other.

I had to give them a break from the game. That's what a bye week is for. Not only to rest your body, but also to rest your mind. And after Monday's practice, these guys needed to do something besides put on pads and slam into each other for two hours.

We also cancelled the Wednesday practice and told the team to rest up. On Thursday, we had a light practice followed by a team meeting.

At this meeting, I started by apologizing to my team for some of the things I had said after the loss to Iowa Tech. I then asked several of our upperclassmen to come up to the front of the room and tell us what they loved about football, what they loved about this school, what they loved about this team, things like that. This talk started out loose and led to several enlightening stories. Eventually, everyone started getting emotional and rebuilding the bonds that were so important for a team to have.

Braxton told us about how his father had been a college football player, but quit after one year. He told Braxton it was the biggest mistake of his life and begged him not to do the same thing. Braxton's father told him to cherish every single moment of "playing the best game God ever invented."

Ray Barnes, a fifth-year senior backup quarterback who would finally be getting the chance to start for us while Jimmy was injured, told the team how he had thought several times about leaving Wisconsin State and transferring to another school where he would have the chance to be more than a backup. "But I could never leave you guys," he said, his eyes getting misty. "I never knew my father and my mother died of a drug overdose when I was in junior high."

The room fell silent.

"I spent high school going from foster home to foster home," Ray continued. "I never had a real family until I came here. You guys are my family now and I could never walk away from you."

Ray had been recruited by the previous staff and I had no idea he had come from such a difficult background. His loyalty to our team touched me. I was far from the only one in the room with tears in his eyes after Ray's talk.

Gavin Smith, a senior defensive end and one of our team captains, told us how he had turned down several scholarship offers from Power Five schools to come to Wisconsin State. He said he chose this school because he wanted to play for the previous head coach, the coach I had replaced. Much to my surprise, he revealed that he had planned on transferring after last season, but his father talked him out of it. Gavin said, "To be honest, I've been unsure about whether I made the right decision to stay here. My heart hasn't been in it. But after tonight, after hearing everybody's stories, for the first time in three years, I can't wait to take the field again with you guys!"

The place erupted after that one.

But the surprise of the meeting came at the end when Coach Chuck DeLuca said he wanted to speak. Chuck was an old-school coach and a man of few words. He never showed much emotion. In fact, I worried that Chuck might be thinking this whole meeting was wasting time that should've been spent on the practice field or in the film room. I couldn't have been more wrong.

Chuck told us that his football career had been cut short by a severe knee injury when he was a senior in high school. He lost all his scholarship offers. "For the longest time," he said, "I would've traded anything to have just one more season, hell, even one more game, as a player. But I can't say that anymore. Because now, there's nothing that thrills me more than seeing you young men go out there and make plays. This, right now, coaching you men, is what I wouldn't trade *anything* for."

The players clapped, but DeLuca wasn't finished.

"You know, people tell me I should retire. I've been doing this for forty years. In fact, I had planned to retire before this season...and the season before, and the season before that. I just can't do it. I can't walk away from the game I love. I can't leave the sounds of the band playing and the pads hitting. I can't walk away from the smell of grass and dirt on a cool fall night in that stadium. I can't leave my fellow coaches. And most of all, I can't leave you guys. I love this game and I love all of you. Don't ever forget that."

The room went nuts.

I saw some of our toughest players weeping like babies that night. Something special had taken place. We had turned an important corner.

For the first time, I saw a level of passion in the eyes of my players that I hadn't seen before. Most importantly, I saw love. Love for the game and love for each other.

13

That week, I also started a new routine. Each morning, as soon as I would wake up, and each night, before falling asleep, I read the words of inspiration that had poured out after my *meetings* with John Wooden and Buck O'Neil. I also wrote the opening lines of those belief statements onto a little card I kept with me. Throughout the day, over and over, I'd repeat them:

1. I focus on only the things I have total control over: my effort and my attitude.

2. I love what I do and I attack each day with joy and enthusiasm.

I was trying to hammer home these principles. Every time I felt myself worrying or slipping into a negative attitude, I repeated the phrases.

I also discussed these statements with my players and coaches. I hung up signs in our locker room that included these two belief statements. I wanted these beliefs to become a part of who we were.

It was working. Everyone was buying in.

In practice, in the weight room, in team meetings, a renewed focus and a sense of positive energy surrounded our team. This powerful new attitude carried into our games.

Even though Jimmy, our starting quarterback, would miss the next three games, Ray Barnes stepped into the role with conviction. He'd been waiting for his chance and he wanted to make the most of it.

I took a lesson from Buck O'Neil and instead of looking at the negatives, I focused on the positives of the situation. Yes, Jimmy was a great quarterback who fit my offensive system perfectly. It was a major obstacle to lose him. But, like Buck said, I had to find the *opportunity* in this obstacle.

Ray was a much different quarterback than Jimmy was. While Jimmy was a pure passer, Ray was more athletic and liked to use his legs to make plays.

In the past, I would have tried to plug Ray into my pass-first system, but he wasn't ready for that. I couldn't force him to be Jimmy. I didn't have another quarterback like Jimmy. So, in the *find the opportunity* line of thinking, I altered my offense to fit better with Ray's skill set. This change would be a surprise to the defenses we faced and it would ultimately make our offense more dynamic.

I lightened up the playbook while adding a few plays designed specifically for Ray. I also adjusted our game plan to include more of a running attack to take some of the pressure off Ray, who would be starting his first college game ever.

Our first game without Jimmy was at home in our conference opener. The Eastern Michigan Eagles were the only MAC opponent we had defeated the previous season. They entered the game with a winless record.

Less than 10,000 fans showed up. It was the smallest crowd in more than twenty years at Wisconsin State.

It was pouring down rain that afternoon and switching our focus to more of a run-oriented attack couldn't have come at a better time. By the fourth quarter, the field was a chewed-up, muddy mess. We rode the backs of our defense and running game to a 26-7 victory.

Ray completed 6-of-12 pass attempts. It was the fewest number of pass plays I'd *ever* called for in a game. He struggled at times, especially early, but relaxed and became more comfortable as the game wore on. He ran for a touchdown late in the fourth quarter to help seal the win for us.

Our next game was against the University of Massachusetts. The UMass Minutemen played in the East Division of the MAC (we played in the West Division) and they were fighting to stay out of the cellar of their division.

We were lucky to start conference play with two of the weaker opponents in the MAC.

Ray played with more confidence this week and I revved up the passing game as he completed 18-of-28 pass attempts while also rushing for 120 yards. He scored once through the air and once on the ground. But the big story was our defense. They forced four turnovers, recorded five sacks, and scored two touchdowns and a safety. We won the game 30-3.

The following week, it was *our* team that struggled to hold onto the football.

Still without Jimmy, we played at Ball State and despite controlling the game for most of the afternoon and racking up 150 more yards than the Cardinals, three crucial turnovers, two missed field goals, and allowing a kick return for a touchdown resulted in us trailing 24-20 with less than three minutes to play.

Starting at our own 12-yard line, Ray was put in a situation he'd never faced before. He would need to lead us down the field with the game on the line.

On the first play of the drive, he dropped back to pass and tried to hit one of our receivers near the sidelines. Ball State's cornerback jumped in front of the ball and it hit him right in the hands…before bouncing to the ground. How he didn't intercept the ball and end the game I'll never know. We survived a big mistake and now had a second chance.

Ray shook off the bad pass and refocused. Over the next three plays, he led us to midfield. There, our offense stalled. After two incomplete passes and a run play that was stopped at the line of scrimmage, I called our final timeout. We faced a fourth-and-ten at the 49-yard line with 24 seconds left in the game.

"Ray," I said, "isn't this fun?"

Ray, who I could tell was nervous, looked at me like I was nuts.

"Isn't this fun?" I repeated. "The game is on the line and *you* have the ball in your hands. This is the type of moment everyone always dreams about when they're kids. This is why you wanted to be a quarterback. Now, you get to live it. It's moments like this that make us all love this great game. Isn't this fun?!"

Ray smiled, stuck out his chest, and held his head high. "You're right, Coach," he said. "This is why God made me!"

As soon as those words left Ray's mouth, I knew we were going to win that game — and so did everyone else on our offense.

On the next play, Ray thought about trying to squeeze in a pass to our tight end, who was closely covered near the first-down marker. Instead, he scrambled away from a defender and bought some more time. He ran to his right and looked downfield just as one of our receivers pulled away from his defender. Ray chucked it deep.

Ray, the kid who I thought didn't have the arm strength to run my pro-style offense, threw a beautiful deep pass that hit his receiver in stride as he crossed the goal line resulting in the game-winning touchdown.

Our defense held on for the final seconds when Ball State got the ball back and we won the game 27-24.

Halfway through our regular season schedule, we were 4-2. After the loss to Iowa Tech, I was certain our season would spiral out of control. What a difference three weeks can make in the life of a college football coach and his team.

14

During my weekly radio show, Randy Tanner said, "Coach, we're happy to see this team on a three-game winning streak, but to be fair, coming into the year we all knew the schedule was back-loaded. Let's be serious, the toughest opponents, with the exception of Michigan State, are waiting for us in the second half of the season. Do you think this team is ready for the next stretch?"

"We don't really think about things like," I said. "We just take it one game at a time."

It was typical coach speak, I know. The type of thing you hear all the time when a coach talks to the media about keeping his team from looking too far ahead. But ever since my conversation with Coach Wooden, I genuinely believed in this approach.

Going into the year, I knew the schedule set up nicely for us to try to build some early momentum. I had worked with our athletic department to design it that way. I was aware that the second half of the year would provide us with our toughest MAC opponents and our in-state "big brother," Wisconsin, but I honestly wasn't thinking about those things now. Thanks to Wooden's rule, I was learning to focus on only the things I had total control over, and that meant getting ready for Northern Illinois.

The Huskies had been champions or co-champions of the MAC West Division for each of the past five seasons. They had won the MAC championship in three of the last four seasons. It had been eight years since Wisconsin State had last defeated Northern Illinois.

Even though the Huskies were favored to beat us by two touchdowns, we had hope that Northern Illinois wasn't as strong as they had been in recent years. They entered the game with an uncharacteristic record of 3-3 and were struggling to get their offense going.

A home crowd of roughly 20,000 fans greeted us for this Saturday-night matchup and we didn't disappoint our fans.

It was one of those games where the Huskies seemed out of rhythm from the beginning. After they went three-and-out on the opening drive, we quickly drove down the field and took the early lead.

Jimmy was back as our starting quarterback and his arm looked great. His passes were crisp and accurate. He also caught a few lucky breaks in the first quarter when two of his passes were tipped by the defense but landed in the hands of one of our receivers.

After building a 14-3 lead and driving, I sent in Ray at quarterback for a change of pace. Sure enough, the defense wasn't ready for his mobility. He busted into the open field on a designed run play and scored a 26-yard touchdown to put us up 21-3.

Being forced to alter my playbook and giving Ray the chance to gain some confidence while Jimmy was hurt had turned out to be a great thing for our offense. We were now able to keep defenses uncomfortable by using two different quarterbacks who had much different playing styles. Jimmy was still our starter, but Ray would now be able to come in for a few plays here and there when we needed to shake things up and confuse the defense.

Northern Illinois was a good team and they found some offensive firepower late in the season, but on this night they played an out-of-character game. We never lost our lead and ended up winning 45-28. It was a game where all the breaks seemed to go our way. I had coached in plenty of games where the opposite had occurred.

Whether our victory was more a matter of us beating the Huskies or the Huskies beating themselves was for the media to discuss. We didn't care. All we could control was how we played and our team basked in the glory of this long-overdue victory against the kings of the conference.

Things were turning our way, but a giant obstacle loomed.

15

It was "Wisconsin Week." Time for another chapter in the semi-regular series between the Wisconsin Badgers and the Wisconsin State Warriors.

Though there were only two FBS college football programs from the state of Wisconsin, Badger fans balked at the idea that anyone would call this game a "rivalry." It was far from a competitive series.

The game was played once every two or three years, always at Wisconsin's Camp Randall Stadium in Madison. The Badgers were the pride of the state. They were the "big brothers" from the Big Ten and we were viewed as their "little brothers" from the MAC, just glad to get invited to play them once in a while.

Wisconsin State had not beaten Wisconsin since 1988, when the Badgers were awful and went 1-10. That season also happened to be the last year Wisconsin State won a MAC title. In other words, it took the perfect combination of Wisconsin having one of their worst seasons in school history and Wisconsin State having their best to pull off the improbable win nearly thirty years ago. The prior

Wisconsin State victory occurred in 1968, when the Badgers happened to go winless. That was it. Just two wins in five decades for the Wisconsin State Warriors in this series.

Heading into the week, the Badgers had a 7-1 record and were ranked number 10 in the nation. We were 24-point underdogs. Nobody thought we had a chance. Myself included.

At our Sunday afternoon coaches meeting, we talked about the best way to handle the big red giant from Madison.

"OK guys, let's talk reality," I said. "We're 5-2 with the final four MAC games all looking to be dogfights. But before we get to those, we have to survive against Wisconsin."

"*Survive*?" Chuck asked.

"Yes, survive," I said. "We're one win away from being bowl eligible and, with Northern Illinois out of the way, we've got a chance to win the division if things fall our way. But we don't have a prayer if we get beat up badly by the Badgers this week. I know this is something none of us want to admit out loud, but we need to install a game plan for getting through the Wisconsin game with as little damage as possible. We can't let the game get ugly. A blowout loss would ruin all the positive momentum we've built up."

I sensed some uneasy body language from my staff.

"I'm not saying the game is over before it begins, I'm just trying to be logical," I said. "We have to think about the season as a whole and what's best for our team."

As I spoke, I realized I was breaking Wooden's advice about keeping the focus on *our* team and not worrying so much about the next opponent. But I needed to be realistic and put my team in the best position to get bowl eligible…and save my job.

"What exactly are you suggesting?" Chuck asked. "We go out there and just run the clock down for four quarters?"

"It sounds bad when you put it like that," I said. "I'm not saying we take a knee on every play, but this is a game where our offense needs to slow things down. We need to run the ball more and milk the clock."

"It's our fast-paced offense that keeps other teams on their heels," our quarterbacks coach said. "Won't we be giving up our biggest advantage if we slow things down?"

"We'll gain an advantage by limiting the number of plays on Saturday," I said. "If we do that, we might catch a few breaks and keep this game close into the fourth quarter. Who knows what could happen then, but we've got to get it into the fourth quarter without things getting out of hand.

"If we run our normal fast and aggressive offense, we run the risk of falling into a big hole early. We do that and we're looking at a possible blowout loss. Not to mention the fact that if we get into a real battle with Wisconsin, we could get beat up pretty bad and suffer some injuries. I don't want to see that happen. We need all hands on deck for the four games *after* Wisconsin."

I saw some reluctant nods.

"Look at it this way," I said. "If we can find a way to win three of our last five games, we're talking about an eight-win season. They can't fire us if we do that. I'm talking about saving our jobs here."

On my way home that night, I stopped at a nearby driving range to hit a bucket of golf balls. Golf had a therapeutic effect on me. Like meditation for some people, the intense focus required to hit that little white ball cleared my mind. I tried to make it a habit of hitting the driving range at least once a week.

But on this night, I wouldn't be hitting any golf balls.

After picking up a bucket of balls in the clubhouse, I walked outside to find the driving range *covered in ice*. This was one of those driving ranges where you hit golf balls into a pond, but the pond had somehow frozen over and walls had been put up around it. The "driving range" had been converted into an ice-skating rink, which didn't make any sense because it wasn't cold enough outside for the pond to freeze over.

A group of men skated back and forth on the ice with hockey sticks in their hands. How was I supposed to hit golf balls onto ice, ice that a dozen or so people were playing hockey on?!

I set down my clubs and my bucket of balls. I looked to my right and left; there weren't any other golfers waiting to tee off.

At that point, I heard a whistle and someone on the ice told everyone, "Take fifteen."

That someone quickly skated my way.

"Excuse me, you're Chris McNeely, right?" he asked as he approached.

I stepped in front of the hitting bay and walked towards the ice. The dark-haired man carried a hockey stick and wore a whistle around his neck. He was obviously a coach here to conduct hockey practice on the frozen pond. He wore a blue jacket with the letters *USA* printed in white on the left side of his chest.

"Yes, that's me," I said. "What in the world is going on here? What happened to the driving range?" I wasn't happy about the fact that my therapeutic golf session had been ruined.

"It's about time you got here," he said. "I've been waiting more than an hour for you." He had the type of

Northern accent that you'd hear more often in places like Minnesota and the Dakotas.

"Oh yeah? How did you know I'd be coming here?"

The man now stood along the outdoor hockey rink's makeshift wall. We were just a few feet away from each other. I vaguely recognized him.

"I was sent here to talk to you. You're about to make a big mistake and I'm here to help make sure you don't follow through with it."

"I don't know what you're talking about, but I'd appreciate it if you moved your team off the ice so I can hit a few golf balls. This is a driving range."

"Not tonight, it isn't."

The nerve of this guy.

"Don't I know you from somewhere?" I asked.

"My name is Herb Brooks," he said. "I'm a hockey coach. You're about to make a big mistake and you don't even realize it."

Herb Brooks wasn't just *a* hockey coach. He was *America's* coach. He famously led the United States hockey team to a win over the "unbeatable" Soviet Union team in the 1980 Winter Olympics. This was the man who engineered "The Miracle on Ice." The man who led a group of young college kids to a shocking gold medal in those

1980 Olympics. The man who had died tragically in a car wreck more than ten years ago.

I didn't waste any more time trying to figure out how this encounter could be possible. After meeting John Wooden and Buck O'Neil, it wasn't such a surprise to be talking with Herb Brooks at a Wisconsin driving range (or, hockey rink) in late October.

What I wondered was *why* he was here. Wooden and O'Neil showed up when I was desperate for answers and searching for help. Brooks was showing up when things were going well for me and our team. I was happy and optimistic about the way our season was going. Why was he showing up now? And what was this mistake he said I was about to make?

16

"I'm honored to meet you, Coach Brooks," I said as I shook his hand.

"Call me Herb." He had a no-nonsense presence, like a man on a mission.

I nodded. "It's truly a pleasure, Herb, but I have to say, I'm confused about why you've been sent here and what problem you think I'm having. For the first time in three years, things are going great for our team. We're on a roll and I'm feeling good about where we are."

Brooks shook his head and said, "That's part of the problem."

"It's a problem to feel good?"

"It's a problem to get complacent," he said. "You're afraid and you're hiding behind complacency."

"Is that right?" I said, rather defensive. "And what am I afraid of?"

"You're afraid of taking risks and dreaming big. You're afraid to see what you've really got. How do I know this? Because I know what you said earlier tonight at your coaches meeting."

"I thought we had a constructive meeting," I said. "We're all excited about the opportunities ahead."

"I wish you could've heard what you sounded like tonight." Brooks looked me straight in the eye. "This talk about winning three out of the next five. Just trying to *survive* this week's game. Changing the game plan so you don't have to risk disappointment. What's the matter with you?"

"I'm trying to be logical and do what's best for the team," I said. "That's my job. How we approach this week's game will have a serious impact on every game that follows."

"You're right about that."

"I'd obviously love to win every one of our games, but we have to be realistic too."

"I'm so tired of hearing that kind of crap," Brooks snapped. "Do you realize how many great things have never been accomplished because somebody decided he needed to be more *realistic*? Do you know how many businesses were never launched, books never written, relationships never started, diseases never cured, and dreams never followed because someone decided he had to be more *logical*?"

He almost seemed angry at me. I put my hands up and smiled, trying to break the tension.

"Herb, take it easy. I'm all about setting big goals and everything, but the goals have to be reasonable--"

"*Reasonable,*" he interrupted. "There's another word people love to throw around when they fear failure, when they fear taking their best shot at life. It's just an excuse to think smaller, to avoid the challenge of thinking bigger and putting yourself on the line.

"McNeely, do you know the difference between being a manager and being a leader?"

He didn't give me a chance to answer.

"I'll tell you what the difference is," Brooks said. "And I'm not talking about job titles. I'm talking about a person's approach to leadership.

"Managing is about maintaining. The manager tries to maintain what is already there. His job is to *manage* what has already been created. He wants to coast. And let me tell you, when you start coasting, there's only one direction you start heading: the *wrong* direction.

"Leading, on the other hand, is about creating something new. A leader must *lead* his people to new heights. A leader moves forward, thinks bigger, and creates a new path—a path that wasn't there before. A leader isn't afraid to dream big even though he must face the unknown and the untried. A leader looks at what he has and asks how he can take it to a whole new level, a level that most people think is *unrealistic* or *unreasonable*.

"Which one are you, McNeely?"

"I'm a leader," I said. "But I also recognize the importance of--"

"--Of being realistic?" Brooks asked rhetorically. "Tell me, how are you being realistic? What's *realistic* about only winning three of your final five games? You just whipped a team that has won your division for five-straight years, you guys are undefeated in your conference, and now you're telling me you think the best you can hope for is going about .500 the rest of the way? What's *realistic* about thinking you have zero shot at beating Wisconsin? Didn't you play Michigan State down to the wire earlier this season? Don't the Badgers only have eighty-five scholarships, just like you? Tell me, how are you being *realistic*?"

"For starters, Wisconsin is the number 10 team in the nation. Our school has *never* beaten a Top 10 team. Never. Beyond that historical fact, Wisconsin is much bigger, stronger, and faster than us and they've only lost to us twice in the last *fifty years*. And, as long as I'm being completely honest here, we needed a last-second touchdown to beat a mediocre Ball State team and I think we caught Northern Illinois on an uncharacteristically bad night for them.

"Don't get me wrong, I'll gladly take those breaks. But the three best teams in our conference are still ahead on the schedule and we're going to need more of those breaks to beat them. I'm not being a negative thinker, I'm being a logical thinker. If I raise expectations to a level our team can't possibly reach, then I'm setting us up for disaster.

"Let's say I tell our guys I think they have what it takes to beat Wisconsin and then we go out there and get blown out. Three years ago, the last time we played those guys, they beat us 51-14. If that happens again, it would devastate our team. Everything we've built up so far this year would be flushed down the toilet.

"Herb, I've seen what happens to teams who go down that path, I've coached them. When I was coaching the Miami Dolphins, I did the whole 'think big' thing. I said we'd win the Super Bowl. I said we'd win regardless of our personnel. I said we'd go undefeated. I said those things and I believed them. You know what happened? As soon as things started going against us, the entire organization turned on me. Everybody—the players, the coaches, the management—*everybody* turns on you. They stop trusting you and those teams never recover. I'm not going to make that mistake again. I've learned to not be so arrogant."

"It's not arrogant to dream big, it's courageous," Herb said. His voice was quieter now. He wasn't mad; he was deeply concerned by what he was hearing.

"McNeely, you didn't lose at Miami because you were dreaming too big. You lost because you put yourself before the people you were supposed to be leading. That's what arrogance is. You can't hide arrogance. Your employees and players see it right away. Thankfully, from what I've seen, you've come a long ways since those days. But don't confuse setting bold goals and high expectations with being arrogant. Those things aren't related one bit."

"Fair point," I said. "But still, I know there's danger in setting up my team with unrealistic expectations."

Herb looked off into the night sky and sighed.

"You're never going to get to where you need to be if you keep thinking like that," he said. "There's a serious problem in American culture today."

That threw me off track. What did my game plan for the Wisconsin game have to do with America's culture?

"It was like this in the seventies too," Herb said.

"You lost me. What exactly are we talking about here?"

"There are some historians who say it was our 1980 hockey team that brought America out of the malaise it was in. Our kids, a bunch of passed-over college hockey players, found a way to beat the greatest hockey team in the world and it encouraged an entire nation to start dreaming big again.

"People forget what it was like back then," Herb continued. "Most the kids who played college hockey in those days were kids who weren't good enough to get drafted into the minor leagues; these were kids most people thought would never be good enough to make a professional team. And professional athletes weren't supposed to play in the Olympics. But the Soviet Union, they had some of the best players in the world and they wouldn't let them come to America to play pro hockey. Instead, they were fulltime pros allowed only to play for Russia. That Soviet Union team may have been the greatest hockey team ever assembled. They beat the NHL All-Star team 6-0 a few months before the Olympic Games started. That's how dominant they were.

"When we beat those guys, when our kids took down the unbeatable Soviets, it sparked something in our country. Suddenly, people realized it was OK to dream big again. What followed was a period of roughly two decades where big-thinking, big-dreaming optimism drove this nation to new heights. Some of the greatest entrepreneurs, innovators, athletes, writers, artists, coaches, and leaders arose out of that period. They made America the world's undisputed leader and more prosperous than ever before.

"I'm not naïve enough to believe our team was the only reason for the boom in optimism and prosperity, but I do think we played a role—even if it was a small one—in helping to ignite that type of thinking once again.

"These days, I feel like our culture has fallen back into a more cynical way of thinking. Too many people are afraid to dream big. They think it's too risky. They're afraid of failing. They're afraid of what other people might say about them. They hide behind excuses like, 'We need to be more realistic.' 'Now is not the time.' 'Our best days are behind us.'"

Herb looked down and shook his head, visibly upset.

"It's really sad," he said. "Polls today show that people think the American Dream is dead. Young people are convinced that their parents and grandparents had it better than they ever will. Can you believe that? That's the epitome of hopelessness.

"What happened to being the country that dreamed big? We set big goals and we went out and accomplished them. We were optimistic. There was *nothing* we couldn't accomplish if we worked hard enough and put our minds to it.

"But then, people got fearful. They started telling themselves they didn't control their own destinies. They started saying the opportunities that existed in the past were long gone. They started blaming everybody else—their neighbors, their parents, the politicians, the rest of the world—for all their problems. Out of fear and resentment, they taught themselves to stop dreaming big, to stop hoping for better days, to stop reaching higher and higher. Instead, they just wanted to get by. To coast. But things only get worse when you adopt that mentality.

"People who think this way are not bad people. They believe they're being practical and choosing safety and security over impractical dreams and ambitions. But there's no such thing as total security. It's a false promise.

"The truth is, when you choose safety and security, you're usually choosing complacency. And when you fall into complacency, you lower your expectations and you give up your biggest dreams. When you settle for mediocrity, you end up with even less. When your goal is to simply *survive*, you'll never *thrive*."

I was beginning to see why Herb Brooks was considered a master motivator.

"Remember this," he said. "At any given time, you're either moving forward or you're moving backward. There is no in-between. There's no such thing as maintaining the status quo. It never works. As soon as you stop trying to move forward and you set your sights on *maintaining*, you start slipping backwards. You're either playing to win or playing not to lose."

"And you think that's what I'm doing with my team?" I asked, though I knew the answer.

"Isn't it obvious?" Herb said. "McNeely, what do you want out of this season? What's your goal with this team? What do you want to achieve?"

"Like Coach Wooden advised, I want my team to be the very best they can be in every practice and game."

"That's good," Herb said. "And are you putting your team in a position to achieve that goal by playing it safe against Wisconsin? McNeely, you'll *never* achieve greatness by playing it safe."

I hadn't thought of it this way. If the goal is to be the very best one can be, then I had to make sure I gave myself and my team the *opportunity* to reach for our highest potential.

"I see what you mean," I said.

"What a person believes is possible will largely determine what it is that person can or cannot do," Herb said. "This is why our dreams and goals are so important. As the leader of your team, you owe it to your players to encourage them to believe bigger. We owe it to our families, our communities, our nation. We owe it to everyone around us. Dreams do come true and we need to become a nation of dreamers once again!

"And yes, you will encounter failures. Let me save you the suspense. When you set big goals and chase big dreams, you will fail along the way, especially at first. That's part of the process. Failure is a necessary step on the path to making big dreams comes true. But failure along the way *confirms* that you're setting big goals, and that's good! Nothing worth doing is ever easy. But with each failure and each setback, you get closer and closer to your ultimate goal.

"Three days before the Olympics started at Lake Placid in 1980, we lost to the Soviets in an exhibition game. They crushed us, 10-3. It might as well have been 20-3. They dominated us in every way. But we learned from it. Past failures lead to future victories *if* you learn from them. When we turned around and beat the Soviets thirteen days after they crushed us, we had to come from behind three times. We had learned how to bounce back from failures. And we recognized the most important lesson anyone can ever learn about failure: the only true failure is giving up.

"Of course, none of that happens if you don't have a big enough dream. If you don't set big, crazy, *unreasonable* goals, you'll never know how far you could've gone.

"McNeely, it takes courage to chase big dreams. It takes courage to set big goals again and again and to keep chasing after them no matter how many times you fall short. To be a leader, you must have the courage to dream big, to commit yourself to those dreams, and to relentlessly pursue those dreams no matter what obstacles you face. Your team, your family, and everyone you come into contact with are all depending on you.

"Have the courage to dream *big*. It's the only way to be a leader. It's the only way to reach your potential and to touch greatness. It's the only way to really feel *alive!*"

It was easy to see why Herb Brooks was able to get so much out of his teams. He exuded passion and intensity. He had a fire to achieve. He had a bring-it-on attitude that was hungry for bigger and more challenging goals.

I wanted to be like that.

We spent more time that night talking about the many obstacles Herb had overcome in his life. The more I learned about that 1980 United States hockey team, the more I realized what a miracle it truly was that those young kids were able to knock off one of the greatest "professional" hockey teams of all time. Anyone being *reasonable, logical*, or *practical* would've said there's no way the Americans could defeat the Soviet Union.

How did they do it? It started with a dream. It started with an idea, planted by Herb, that the Soviets *could* be defeated. And Herb convinced his players that destiny had tapped them to be the team that would finally beat the Soviets.

Herb believed it, his players believed it, and it happened.

"You can't listen to the naysayers," Herb said. "They may mean well, but all they do is tell you why something can't be done. It's amazing what you can achieve when you start focusing on the reasons why you *can* do something instead of the reasons why you can't."

This comment hit me hard. I had been so focused on all the reasons we didn't have a shot against Wisconsin and all the things that could go wrong if we got blown out by the Badgers. I realized then it was time to start focusing on all the reasons we *could* pull off the big upset.

Just before Herb went back to his practice on the frozen pond, I had to ask him one more question. That 1980 team was known as "The Miracle on Ice." Al Michaels, the announcer for the game, had perhaps the most famous line in sports broadcasting history when he called out, "Do you believe in miracles? Yes!" during the final seconds of play in the victory against the Soviets.

"Herb, do you believe in miracles?"

He smiled, acknowledging that he'd probably been asked that question a thousand times.

"I do," he said. "But I believe most miracles happen from within. They start inside us. They start with a dream, a belief that it *can* be done, followed by extremely hard work and perseverance.

"But without the dream first, the miracle will never happen."

17

As soon as I rolled out of bed the next morning, I grabbed a pen and let the words flow:

I DREAM BIG AND I IGNORE THE NAYSAYERS. I set huge goals and I fully commit myself to achieving those goals. I ignore those who tell me to be more "realistic" about my goals. Naysayers represent the voices of fear and cynicism and I will not listen to them. I remind myself of all the reasons my dreams CAN come true. I will become the best version of myself and the only way to reach my full potential is to aim as high as possible. Every day, a person makes the choice to either move forward or backward. Today, I choose to move forward and chase my biggest dreams. Miracles will occur when I work hard to follow MY dreams.

I also added Herb's lesson to the card I carried with me, which now read:

1. I focus on only the things I have total control over: my effort and my attitude.

2. I love what I do and I attack each day with joy and enthusiasm.

3. I dream big and I ignore the naysayers.

When I got to the office, I immediately called a coaches meeting.

"Change of plans," I said. "We're not going to *survive* against Wisconsin this Saturday. We're going to give it *everything* we have and find a way to make history on Saturday!"

"Now we're talking!" said one assistant as he banged his fist on the desk. "Let's do this." The response from all the coaches confirmed this was the right strategy.

We then had a brainstorming session on how to attack the Badgers and try to confuse them with our offense and take away their strengths on defense. The game plan we put together sounded plausible.

We were starting to believe.

After the meeting, Chuck stayed back to tell me, "I don't know what caused your change of heart, but I'm on board all the way."

The coaching staff's enthusiasm spilled into practices and film sessions that week. It was infectious. By Friday, every player on our team had the champion's look in their eyes. They believed.

During our Friday night team meeting, we went through all the reasons we *could* beat Wisconsin. We went over and over them. Not once did we mention one of *their* strengths, *their* winning streak against us, or the fact that *they* were a Top 10 team. It was all about why *we* could do the seemingly impossible.

On Saturday afternoon, in front of 80,000 fans in Madison, we went out and made history.

The Badgers came out for the 11 a.m. kickoff lethargic and, dare I say, *complacent*. We made them pay for it on our first drive as Jimmy led our fast-paced offense to a 7-0 lead less than five minutes into the game.

We forced a Wisconsin punt on their first series and picked up a field goal on our next drive to take a 10-0 lead midway through the first quarter. The Badgers woke up after that and came charging back.

By halftime, tenth-ranked Wisconsin had regained the lead 21-17. They returned the second-half kickoff deep into our territory and scored three plays later to go up 28-17.

For a moment, it looked like the Badgers would be pulling away and burying Wisconsin State like they always did. But we answered with a 95-yard touchdown return on the ensuing kickoff, which breathed new life into our team.

The rest of the afternoon was a back-and-forth tug-of-war for momentum. Wisconsin relied on a bruising running game while we dinked and dunked our way down the field with quick passes. Every once in a while, I'd take Jimmy out and put in Ray to run a few plays at quarterback, but the Badgers knew what we were doing and they shut Ray down as a rushing threat.

With ten minutes left to play in the game, we got the ball back at our own 7-yard line. Backed up against our end zone, we trailed 38-34. Instead of playing it safe with a conservative run call or short pass, I decided it was time to swing for the fences. We ran a play-action pass that let Jimmy throw the ball deep downfield. The one-on-one coverage was good, but the Badgers' cornerback lost the ball in the sun just as it arrived. He lost his balance and fell to the ground as our receiver reeled in the ball and took it all the way for a 93-yard touchdown.

The stadium was silent except for the rambunctious upper corner where a few thousand of our fans celebrated.

We had regained the lead for the first time since the opening quarter and we didn't give it up. Wisconsin missed a long field goal attempt as time expired.

The final score: Wisconsin State 41, No. 10 Wisconsin 38.

It was our school's first win ever against a team ranked in the Top 10 and the first time we had defeated our in-state opponent from the mighty Big Ten in nearly three decades.

How different the result could've been if I had stuck with my original game plan and been afraid to dream big.

When we arrived back on our campus, several thousand fans were there to greet us. The university and the town partied all through the night. This is what college football is all about.

When I finally made it back home, I was surprised to see that Cindy wasn't sharing my joyous mood.

"What's wrong?" I asked. "Don't you realize what this means for our future?"

"Yes, I do," she said. "And that's the problem."

"The *problem*?"

"All night I've been listening to reporters argue about your future. They're saying we won't be here next year because bigger and better schools will be calling."

I burst out laughing. "Three months ago those shows wouldn't shut up talking about how they needed to run us out of town. Now they're arguing about whether they can keep us here?"

"Even somebody on ESPN was talking about you. They said you'll be a dark-horse candidate for any team that needs to rebuild their offense."

"I'm sorry, hon, but I'm failing to see how any of this is a bad thing."

"Chris, I don't want to leave Wisconsin State." She had tears in her eyes. "I love it here. I want to raise our daughter and our *son* here."

"Son? We're having a boy?!"

"We're having a boy," Cindy said.

I hugged Cindy and didn't want to let go. At this point, we both had tears in our eyes.

For the first time in a long time, I loved my life again. We had righted the ship. The turnaround was complete and things were only going to get better from here.

That's how it felt that night, at least.

But a lot can change in a week.

18

Less than twenty-four hours after the biggest win in the history of Wisconsin State Warriors football, I had already shifted my focus to the next game. We'd be traveling to face Bowling Green. After a slow start to the season, the Falcons had caught fire and won seven games in a row. With a 7-2 record, Bowling Green was undefeated in conference play and they were the MAC East Division's top team.

At my weekly press conference on Monday, I was asked by a reporter if I had been contacted by any other schools about their coaching vacancies.

"No, I haven't," I said, which was the truth.

"Some have speculated that you could be a candidate for the Illinois job," another reporter said. "Is that something you're interested in?" Illinois, a Big Ten school, had recently fired their head coach.

"To be honest, right now, I'd just like to be offered a contract extension from Wisconsin State," I said with a smile.

Judging by the smatter of whispers, this information came as a surprise to the media.

"You mean you haven't been offered an extension?" a reporter yelled at.

"Uh, actually, these are matters I'd prefer to keep private and I haven't thought much about them," I said, trying to change the subject. "My focus is 100 percent on Bowling Green right now."

Friday morning, I got a call from Larry Wilcox. He was Wisconsin State's athletic director, my boss. Larry asked me to stop by Ted Mueller's home. Ted was one of the school's wealthiest and most influential donors. When he wanted a meeting with the head coach, he got one.

I arrived at Ted's massive estate and was welcomed to his game room, where he was shooting pool and drinking a cocktail at eleven in the morning.

"Chris, thank you for making the time to come see me," Ted said.

"It's no problem at all," I fibbed.

"I wanted to talk to you about something before you left for Bowling Green. It's about what you said at Monday's press conference."

It was time for contract extension talks to begin. Finally.

"I misspoke," I said. "I shouldn't have talked about my contract in public. But now that you mention it, I'm glad we're having this conversation."

Ted raised his eyebrows and gave me an amused look.

"As I'm sure you can understand," I continued, "I'll have to listen to any offers that come my way, especially from Power Five schools, but I want you to know that Cindy and I have been talking about it and we're still very interested in staying at Wisconsin State if we can work something out. We like it here."

"Oh, really?" Ted said with a sly grin. "How noble of you to consider staying at little ol' Wisconsin State. But what makes you think *we* want you to stay here?"

I forced an uncomfortable chuckle. "I guess I just assumed that's what you wanted to talk to me about."

"Chris, that was a fantastic win you pulled off last week. I didn't think you had it in you. None of us did."

I wanted to know who the "us" he was referring to was, but didn't ask.

"We're all very proud of what you did." He took a sip of his drink and looked me in the eye. "But the thing is, wheels have already been set in motion. Know what I mean?"

"No, not really," I said.

"After that ugly Iowa Tech loss, I started making some calls. You understand, I'm sure. We've got a new guy in mind for our Warriors. A guy I've known all my life. Frankly, it's someone I've *dreamed* of bringing to Wisconsin State for the past ten years or so. And, like I said, the wheels are already in motion. One big win just isn't enough to stop that motion. Make sense?"

"You're saying you've already offered *my* job to a new candidate, some old pal of yours?"

Ted smiled and slammed his pool stick into the cue ball, which knocked another ball perfectly into the corner pocket.

"You got it," he said. "It's nothing personal. It's just that we don't think you're the right fit for Wisconsin State. I wanted to be upfront with you and tell you this face-to-face, man-to-man. That way, you can stop fighting for your job at press conferences. I don't want you looking desperate and making a fool of yourself in front of the media."

My blood boiled. "And you speak for the athletic department?"

"I can," Ted said with a confident smirk. "And I do."

"I don't understand, this doesn't make any sense. We've got a chance to win our division and the conference. We could win ten games this year. That's *never* happened at this school. Seems like an odd time to fire somebody."

"I don't see it as *firing* you. We're just...letting your contract expire. After all, you're the one who wanted a three-year contract when you came here, remember? And besides, I'm sure you'll land on your feet. Though you and I both know none of the Power Five schools are calling, I'm sure you can probably land a job with another MAC school or get in as a coordinator somewhere. That's probably what you're best suited for, being a coordinator again. Don't you think?"

I shook my head and headed for the door.

"Chris, don't take it personally."

I stopped and turned to face Ted. I wanted to say a million different things to this guy, but I also didn't want to give him the satisfaction of seeing me fight for my job.

"Just out of curiosity, what is your reasoning?" I asked. "How can you sell this to the administration after what we did on Saturday?"

Ted flashed an arrogant smile and sighed. "You and I both know you pulled off a freakin' *miracle* on Saturday. And before that, you caught Northern Illinois off guard during one of their worst seasons in a long time. With the four teams left on the schedule, you'll be lucky to win another game. By the time it's all said and done, you might not even make it to a bowl game.

"Tell you what, though," Ted said in his condescending tone. "I'll still make a few calls for you, make sure you land on your feet somewhere. How's that sound?"

I left without responding.

I didn't tell anyone about the conversation. I was fuming. I couldn't sleep at the team hotel the night before the Bowling Green game. One overwhelming thought repeated itself again and again throughout the night: *What's the point? What difference does any of this make if they've already decided to fire me?*

All day on Saturday, I tried unsuccessfully to ignore a series of negative thoughts that kept running through my head: *How could this be? I had worked so hard to get this thing turned around and it was all for nothing! How could they want to let me go after the way we've been playing? No matter what we do the rest of the season, my fate has already been decided. This isn't right! Why didn't Larry, my boss, have the guts to tell me this? Why did he make me meet with Ted and sit through his smugness? Was there something more going on here? Was somebody out to get me? Why was I being treated this way? Was I toxic person? Did people simply not like working with me?*

I couldn't focus on the game. Despite a solid effort by our defense for three quarters, my offensive play-calling was out of rhythm all afternoon.

The Falcons scored three fourth-quarter touchdowns to beat us handily, 38-10.

As I walked off the field that afternoon, I could just imagine Ted's big grin as he told one of the other boosters, "See, I told you the win over Wisconsin was a fluke."

I was mad at myself for letting the conversation with Ted bother me so much. In the worst way possible, I had violated Wooden's rule about focusing on only what I could control: my effort and my attitude in the present moment. My lack of focus had cost us the game. It wasn't fair to the players. They deserved my best and I let them down.

I was also disgusted by the way the college-donor system was working against me. Why did a guy like Ted Mueller have so much control over *my* destiny? I started questioning whether I had what it took to stay in this profession. This was a direct violation of Buck O'Neil's lesson about loving what you do and focusing on the positives in every situation.

Herb Brooks had taught me to dream big and ignore the naysayers. Here I was, letting one single naysayer rob me of my confidence and question my abilities.

What if Ted is right? What if we've been a fluke up to this point and we're about to get slammed back to reality over the final few weeks of the season? If that happens, who would want to hire me as their next coach, a guy who took over a winning program and finished his three seasons with a losing record?

Not only was I already broke, but I was certain I'd soon be unemployed as well.

19

On the somber plane ride back to Wisconsin State after our humiliating loss to Bowling Green, my anger, my self-doubt, and the series of negative thoughts running through my head led me to an epiphany: *I was done with this job.*

It was time for me to retire from coaching. I would offer my resignation on Monday and I wouldn't give people like Ted, Larry, or the rest of the boosters who wanted me gone the satisfaction of *getting* to fire me.

I was 39 years old; I had plenty of time to start a new life. This career wasn't enjoyable to me anymore. The lows after losses were five times worse than the highs after winning. Dealing with people like Ted took the fun out of this game. The stress and pressure was all just too much. I could no longer handle the vitriol and uncertainty that came with this job. There had to be a better way. It was time to do something different with my life.

I still loved the game, but the game didn't love me back.

It may seem like this was a rash decision, just one week removed from the biggest win of my career and feeling like my life was on the right track again, but I didn't see it that way. The weeks prior to the Bowling Green game had been the *exception* and not the rule. I could see that now. Over the past three years, the bad times had far outweighed the good times. It was time for me to face reality. I wasn't cut out for this profession.

I was done.

Late that night, after all the other coaches had gone home, I sat down in my office to write my resignation letter. An icy rain was clacking against the window as I struggled to find the right words.

I called Cindy and told her I'd be working late and might not make it home tonight. I couldn't face her. I didn't know how to tell her I'd made up my mind to retire from coaching. I didn't want her to try to talk me out of it. My decision had been made. Would she be scared about our future? She'd certainly want to know what I planned on doing next, and I had no idea. I also knew how angry she'd be when she found out that my fate at Wisconsin State had been decided weeks ago and that no matter what we did, I would not be invited to stay in the community she had fallen in love with.

Though I felt certain in my decision to walk away from coaching, I didn't feel the sense of relief I thought I should. I was still too angry. I couldn't stop my mind from racing in all directions. I sat with pen in hand and stared at the blank page on my desk. I couldn't write a single word.

When things are going bad, it can be so hard to stop stewing and focus on something constructive.

My passion for the game I loved had finally been extinguished by people like Ted, by the insensitive and mean-spirited fans who called into sports talk shows to rip on me as a coach and as a person, and by the losses that piled up and wore me down. I just didn't have it in me to bounce back when things kept crashing down again and again, harder and harder every time.

It was time to retire. There had to be an easier way to make a living.

My eyes glazed over. I started to nod off and shook myself awake. I looked over at the corner couch I'd spent too many nights on. *Not tonight*, I decided. I needed to go home; I needed a real bed and a good night's sleep.

I stumbled down the hallway in a sleepy fog and when I stepped outside, two things jumped out at me.

First off, the icy rain had stopped falling. In fact, it was now as bright as the midafternoon and so hot I thought I'd stepped into an oven. The sound of cicadas added to the summerlike setting. I started sweating profusely in my warm winter jacket.

Secondly, our grass practice field, which I passed by every day, was no longer the lush green color I was used to. It looked like it hadn't been watered in months. There were barren dirt patches and the grass that was there had been scorched yellow and brown.

For a moment, I thought I was losing my mind — something to do with sleep deprivation, perhaps. But then I realized what was happening.

Alone in the middle of a dirt patch near midfield was a John Wayne-like figure, standing there puffing on a cigarette, unbothered by the blazing sun. He was wearing a crimson sport coat and his famous houndstooth hat.

The man they call the greatest coach in the history of college football had come to pay me a visit.

20

Paul "Bear" Bryant looked my way, made eye contact, and turned away with a grimace. He didn't call out my name, he didn't smile, he didn't walk towards me, and he didn't wave me over. He gazed back across the patchy field and just stood there, almost as though he was ignoring me, hoping I might not come talk to him.

But I couldn't pass up an opportunity to talk with this legend, even if he wasn't exactly welcoming.

I took off my winter jacket, tossed it to the ground, and made my way toward the Bear. With each step I took, the hard, dry grass cracked underneath me and smoky dust kicked up.

"Coach Bryant," I said, as soon as I was close enough for him to hear me, "You've always been a hero of mine. I can't tell you what a thrill this is to meet you."

Bear didn't look my way. He took a final drag off his cigarette, dropped it onto the dirt, and smashed it into the ground with his shoe.

"So you want to quit?" he said. His Southern drawl was deep, slow, and gravely. He made it clear he despised even saying the word *quit*.

"*Retire* is the word I would use," I said.

"I usually don't talk to quitters, but I guess I *have* to talk to you."

"I'm *retiring*, not quitting," I stressed. "I've thought about it and it's time."

Bear huffed. Even his exhale was deep and scratchy.

"You've thought about it, huh?" he asked. "For what, a whole plane ride home after a tough loss?"

"I know it seems like that, but it's a culmination of everything that has happened over the past three years. Actually, everything that's happened over the past ten years. It's just not worth it anymore. I've lost the passion. I'm done."

"Son, I think you better think this through a little longer. We all hate losing, but it's part of the game. And good decisions are rarely made when we feel bad about ourselves. I also understand you didn't sleep a wink last night. Being tired makes cowards of us all. You need to think about this idea of yours."

He finally looked at me, like he was studying me for a moment.

"I don't think you're a quitter," Bear said. "You just haven't learned what it takes to be a champion."

"I know you have to love what you do to be really great at it and I can tell you that I've lost my passion for this game."

"What a load of B.S.," Bear growled. "You *love* this game, son. It's in your blood. It consumes you night and day. I know it does. Can you think of any other career that could consume your mind and spirit the way coaching football does?"

"I do love football, sure, but it's the baggage that comes with it that I can't take anymore. So much stress and uncertainty."

"You mean pressure," he said. "You think the pressure is too much for you to handle, don't you?"

"I guess so," I said, trying to be honest with a man who clearly despised signs of weakness in the face of pressure.

"Let me tell you something, there's going to be pressure with anything you do," Bear said. "Life is full of pressure. There are going to be ups and downs with any career you choose. And if it's not with your career, it's going to be health issues, trouble with your kids, trouble with your wife, trouble with your neighbor, trouble with your car, trouble with the weather. There's *always* going to be something and quitting the job you love ain't going to change that."

Bear moved slowly and talked slowly, he made you wait on his words.

"And since there's going to be pressure and stress with anything, that's all the more reason you should stick with something you love doing," he said. "If it's all going to be hard anyway, you might as well pick something you enjoy. Don't you think?"

"But that's the problem," I said. "I *don't* enjoy it anymore. It's worn me down to the point that I don't think I can keep doing it. It's time for a change."

Bear shook his hand and looked across the ugly field again.

"Do you know where you are?" he asked.

"I'm definitely not in Wisconsin anymore," I said.

"This is the field where I held training camp for my favorite team ever, the 1954 Texas A&M Aggies. This is Junction, Texas. Do you know the story behind this place?"

I nodded. Most football coaches knew the legend of *The Junction Boys*.

The story goes like this. When Bear Bryant was hired at Texas A&M, he inherited a losing team loaded with "legacy" players. In the days before strict scholarship limits, it wasn't uncommon for large college programs to have well over 100 football players on scholarship. The Aggies had given these scholarships away liberally, often handing them out to the sons and friends of previous A&M players or those connected to the program in some way. Many of these legacy players weren't good enough to deserve the scholarships they received.

Bear took a look at what he was inheriting at A&M and realized he needed to clean house if he was going to build a championship program. So, he decided to hold preseason camp in the secluded town of Junction, Texas, which was located 250 miles away from campus. The town was in the middle of a multiyear drought when Bear decided to hold his 1954 camp there and the temperature regularly exceeded 100 degrees during this stretch.

He put his team through hell. Grueling marathon practice sessions followed by nonstop team meetings. The players had to sleep on bunks crowded into tin-roof barracks that felt hotter inside than outside.

One-hundred-and-fifteen Aggies made the trip to Junction. Only thirty made it back. The rest had quit the team.

That 1954 team, with such a small roster of players, went 1-9. It was Bryant's only losing season in his 38 years as a head coach. However, the Junction survivors paved the way for an undefeated season just two years later, in 1956.

Despite a career that included coaching six national championship teams, Bear Bryant's only losing team was his favorite.

"The boys that survived my camp here were the epitome of perseverance." Bear said. "It's amazing what can happen when a man *decides* he won't give up. You wouldn't believe how much further his limitations can be stretched."

Bear looked at me, as though he was wondering how I could even think about quitting after what he saw his '54 Aggies endure.

"That's the one thing that separated my teams from everybody else's." He paused, as though he was about to reveal the secret to success. "Mental toughness. My teams were relentless. In practice, I pushed them to the edge of where they *thought* they could go and then pushed them further and further past that. They learned that their ability to handle pressure and adversity was limited only by their beliefs. That's what mental toughness is all about."

"Sounds sort of like Navy SEALs training," I said.

"It is sort of like that. Most people have no idea how much pressure they can take, how many obstacles they can withstand, how many times they can get knocked down and still get back up. They don't realize how far they can be pushed because they place mental limits on themselves.

They quit before they ever come close to reaching their true potential.

"And the sad thing is, once you start backing down, it gets easier and easier to give up. When you quit the first time, it's hard. The second time, it gets easier. The third time, you don't even have to think about it. Quitting then becomes a way of life."

I looked down, knowing he was right. I'd never quit anything before and here I was, ready to do exactly what I always taught my players *not* to do.

"Why do I love that first Texas A&M team so much, even though they only won one game that season?" Bear asked. "Because the boys that made it through that camp never, ever quit. Sure, we lost nine games that year, but I can handle losing as long as I know my boys didn't quit. And those kids *never* quit. It was one of the greatest things I've ever seen."

Bear shook his head as he thought about them. It was as though that team represented a moment where even he couldn't believe how much they withstood and still refused to quit.

"I would tell all my teams, 'Winning isn't imperative, but getting tougher in the fourth quarter is,'" Bear said. "That's what mattered most to me.

"It all starts with the belief that you *can* handle whatever challenge you're facing. You *can* go further. You *can* withstand any trouble that comes your way.

"If you believe that, *if you believe that deep in your gut,* then nothing can beat you down. Nothing at all."

"That all *sounds* great," I said, "And we all want to be that relentless in life, but most of the players didn't survive your Junction training camp. Most people don't make it through Navy SEALs training. If it's all mental, what makes the difference between those who quit and those who stick it out?"

"Simple. It's a *choice* each man makes. I've seen plenty of quitters in my time, plenty of kids who never gave me their all and never reached their God-given potential. Over the decades, I developed a pretty good eye for those who had the mental toughness to succeed and those who didn't. Those who were willing to *choose* perseverance and those who I could tell would be looking to quit as soon as the going got tough. I passed up on loads of much more talented recruits because I knew they didn't have the mental toughness required to play on one of my teams."

"How could you tell who had it and who didn't?" I asked.

"I never knew for certain, of course, but if I saw too much complacency or too much self-doubt, I knew I wouldn't be able to get the best out of them no matter how hard I tried. They had already developed a habit of quitting on themselves. That's why I always liked undersized, scrappier kids. I knew they had something to prove. I knew they had been told over and over again that they didn't have what it took, but they refused to believe it.

"I always liked to tell people, 'It's not the size of the dog in the fight, but the size of the fight in the dog.'"

"I think I've heard that one," I said with a smile, acknowledging the quote that had become so famous in coaching circles.

Bear offered the hint of a smile and continued. "The important thing to understand is that after four decades of coaching, I saw confirmed time and time again what I always knew to be true. And that is this: *mental toughness is a choice you make*. It's not some gift that some people have and some don't. It's a choice. And the choices a man makes become a habit. Unfortunately, most people *choose* to get in the habit of quitting."

"And how did you teach those with potential to become more mentally tough?" I asked. "This world can be a cruel place. How did you teach people to form the habit of persevering?"

"Lots of ways.

"The first thing you have to do is recognize that setbacks are only temporary. The pain of a hard day's practice is temporary. The disappointment of a loss is temporary. The problem that came out of nowhere is temporary. Tough times never last and champions recognize that. They know that adversity is temporary and limited in scope. They keep the big picture in mind. They remind themselves that if they can power through the temporary tough times, the ultimate reward will be worth it.

"Quitters, on the other hand, see a setback as permanent, something that will never end. This false belief discourages them and makes it easy to quit. They figure, 'What's the point of trying if it's never going to get better?' They also tend to blow up problems and make them much bigger than they really are. In the eyes of a quitter, every small problem suddenly becomes a catastrophe that affects every area of their life. The mentally tough don't do that. They know the problem is only temporary and that it'll soon pass if they keep moving forward and attacking it head-on.

"Another thing the mentally tough don't do is make excuses or blame other people for their problems. Instead, they accept full responsibility for where they are and where they're going. They don't blame their competition, they don't blame God, they don't blame their parents, or their bosses, or their coworkers, or their boosters. They take charge and accept full responsibility for righting the ship themselves. Even if the cause of the problem *was* somebody else's fault, the mentally tough still don't waste time making excuses about what shoulda, coulda, or woulda happened had things gone down differently. No, they don't waste time and energy on excuses and regrets. They charge forward.

"I used to tell people, 'If anything goes bad, I did it. If anything goes semi-good, we did it. If anything goes real good, you did it.' That's what being a leader means. The buck stops with *you* when there are problems. No excuses. No blaming others."

"Lately, I've been guilty of that," I admitted.

"The world doesn't owe you a thing," Bear said. "Realize this from now on and it'll save you a lot of heartache. Like Buck O'Neil told you, you have to go out there and get what you want. You can't wait around for someone to hand it to you."

I nodded.

"Another area I've struggled a lot with lately is anger," I said. "Some people or some circumstances make me so angry that I lose my focus and can't concentrate on moving forward.

"For instance, I haven't been able to stop boiling about the booster who told me there was no way I could keep my job, even after we've been playing well! How can that be fair? It's just wrong to treat people like that."

"Anger is good," Bear said with a smile.

"How is it *good* to be angry?" I asked.

"The mentally tough learn how to take their anger and use it as fuel for accomplishing a goal. You talked to Herb Brooks, right? One of the ways he motivated his 1980 U.S. hockey team was getting the players so angry at him that they came together as a team and let go of their petty inner-squad rivalries. It was a brilliant tactic. And it's a good example of how you can use anger to fuel your performance and motivate you forward.

"Another way is to take something that is making you angry, something like an unjust situation or a double-cross or just plain bad luck, and use it to fuel your focus. Take this booster who's got you all bent out of shape. Why would you quit and let him get the last laugh by forcing you to quit? Why would you stew about him and let him steal your focus to the point that you can't give your best moving forward?"

"I'm trying not to," I said. "But it's easier said than done."

"Isn't everything?" Bear said. "Stop trying and start doing. Decide that you won't let him rob you of your passion and your focus. Instead, use that anger to keep yourself focused on proving him wrong, showing him what you can do. Every time you start to stew about what he said to you, what he's trying to do to you, or what you imagine him doing next, immediately shift your focus to *proving him wrong*. I'm telling you, it works. Take your anger and use it as motivation to make yourself so good that he can't deny you what you earn. Take your anger and use it to your advantage!"

"That's an interesting way to handle it," I said. "I kept trying to ignore him and the things he said, but every time I tried to ignore it, it only made things worse."

"And that's the problem. Don't try to ignore or bury that anger, *use* it as motivation."

I nodded; this sounded like a much more productive approach than stewing about the things that made me angry.

Bear's demeanor turned warmer as saw he was getting through to me. He put a hand on my shoulder and shared several stories of guts and grit as we walked along the scorched practice field.

"Another thing you have to do if you want to be mentally tough is *expect* problems," he said. "I know that goes against a lot of the feel-good positive thinking stuff you hear these days. And don't get me wrong, it *is* important to have a positive attitude. But a positive attitude is about knowing problems will come up and that you have what it takes to overcome them. Too many people think that if you just think positive thoughts, nothing bad will ever happen. Those folks have it all wrong. That's not positive thinking, that's wishful thinking. And if you think that way, that you're entitled to a life where nothing ever goes wrong, you're going to be blindsided and unprepared when life throws trouble your way.

"A positive attitude won't prevent you from facing obstacles. What a positive attitude will do is help you blast through those obstacles.

"Mental toughness isn't about avoiding problems; it's about fighting through them. You have to have a can-do, bring-it-on type of attitude. Don't make the mistake of thinking you can somehow avoid all problems. If you think like that, you'll run for the hills as soon as things go wrong.

"Expect problems and then expect to overcome them."

As we walked, Bear told me how he used his dirt-poor childhood as motivation to prove he could be somebody. Growing up, he was told he'd never amount to anything. It made him angry and that anger was the fuel he used to prove everyone wrong.

Bear told me about the time when he was 13 years old and a carnival came to town with a guy offering five bucks to anyone who would wrestle his muzzled bear. Bryant accepted the challenge. And though the guy left town without paying up, Paul Bryant earned one of football's greatest nicknames on that day.

He told me about the time he played a full game on a broken leg against Tennessee. "And, by God, it was probably the best game I ever played," Bear said about the incident.

Bear explained how he would tell his players that if they could survive four years in his program without quitting, they'd never quit anything in their life. Everything he did was designed to get more out of his players, more than they thought was possible. Again and again, he'd push them to the edge...and then just a little further.

He told me how he used to demote or even cut star players to see how they responded. He wanted to crush any sense of entitlement or complacency and reignite a fire in them.

Bear reiterated again and again that mental toughness was a choice. Each person must *choose* to persevere and never give up. Because Bear was so certain that perseverance was based on a choice people could freely make for themselves, he had very little respect for those who quit on their dreams.

"The longer I coached, the more I realized that different players responded to different types of motivation," Bear said. "Some kids responded best to a kick in the pants, getting called out and having their toughness challenged. Others kids responded best to a pat on the back, getting reassured that I believed in them and knew they could go further. But regardless of the motivational tactic they responded best to, my job was to teach them how to *choose* perseverance in the face of adversity. My job was to push them to the breaking point where they had to choose between pressing forward or backing down.

"What I learned is that it's *always* a choice. That's why it drives me crazy to see someone quit. They've willingly chosen to settle, to back down, to give up. Nothing makes me more disappointed."

Bear looked down in disgust before continuing.

"The thing is, Chris, everybody gets knocked down, but champions *choose* to get back up. They *choose* to never back down and never stop trying.

"Until you believe that, and I mean truly believe in your heart that perseverance is a choice you make, well then, you'll always be on the verge of quitting. You'll be one little setback away from quitting on yourself, your family, and your dreams.

"Do you want to be that type of person?" Bear asked me, now looking me directly in the eye.

"Of course not," I said.

"That's what I thought," Bear said with a slap on my back. "You want the secret to success in this life? Here it is: Make the decision to never, never, never, *never* give up on your goals and dreams. Simple as that.

"When a man decides he will never give up, he *assures* himself of success. It sounds simple, but it's the truth.

"You mentioned uncertainty as a reason you wanted to leave coaching. Son, the only way to be certain about anything is to make a total commitment to never giving up. That's the only way to be *certain* that you'll succeed. There's no magic formula, just good old fashioned grit and determination.

"If you make that commitment to never quit, you'll carry a mental edge with you wherever you go. You'll *know* that nothing can stop you. You'll *know* that your success is certain in the long run.

"No matter what adversity you face, no matter how hard everyone else tries to push you down, no matter how many times you get knocked off course, you've got to make the commitment that it will *never* be enough to get you to quit. Make the commitment to being unstoppable and there's no limit to what you can accomplish."

"It's my choice," I said. "Nobody else's."

"Damn right," Bear said with a grin. "I've had this conversation enough times over the decades to know when

I'm getting through to someone and when I ain't. You, son, are buying in. I can see it in your eyes. You ain't quitting nothing."

Bear checked his watch and abruptly said, "Now, I've got to get going, I've got some film to watch."

"Some film?" I asked as Bear began walking away. "You're still coaching?"

"Of course," he said. "I'll never quit."

He'd been dead for more than three decades and yet this man was still consumed by the game he loved.

"Do you ever stop working, Coach?"

He looked back with a smile. "Hell, no. Work is fun to me, son. What could be better than football?"

Buck O'Neil would appreciate hearing that response.

21

The next morning, instead of writing a resignation letter, I wrote the following:

I AM RELENTLESS AND I WILL NEVER GIVE UP ON MY DREAMS. I know that problems will come my way, but I know that I have what it takes to overcome each and every one of them. No matter what obstacles I face today, I will fight my way through them. Nothing can stop me from reaching my chosen destination. I CHOOSE to persevere and never back down from the obstacles that stand between me and my dreams. Simply making this decision to never give up ASSURES me of success in whatever I set out to do. I will never, ever give up on my dreams. I am unstoppable.

The card I carried with me now contained four belief statements:

1. I focus on only the things I have total control over: my effort and my attitude.

2. I love what I do and I attack each day with joy and enthusiasm.

3. I dream big and I ignore the naysayers.

---

4. I am relentless and I will NEVER give up on my dreams.

When I met with the team for our Monday-morning meeting to start the week, I could sense that the players' confidence had been rattled after the beat-down we'd experienced at Bowling Green. They were questioning their abilities, wondering where we go from here. I could see it in their eyes.

"Men," I told them, "You play for the Wisconsin State *Warriors*. That word, *warrior*, should mean something special to you. As a member of this football team, you must become a warrior. And to become a warrior, you must adopt a warrior's mindset.

"What does it mean to have a warrior's mindset? It means that we go into battles knowing that sometimes we will win and sometimes we will lose. But regardless of the outcome, a warrior never, ever, ever gives up or backs down from the next fight. A warrior *never* quits. A warrior must make the decision that no matter what challenge he is currently facing or what setback he went through in the past, he is going to charge ahead again and again with reckless abandon.

"It doesn't matter how many times the warrior gets knocked down, he will *always* get back up. Again and again and again."

I saw some heads nodding.

"A warrior isn't made when everything is going his way," I continued. "A warrior is born in the face of adversity. It's all about attacking the next fight, the next battle, the next game, the next practice, and the next play. No matter what has happened in the past, warriors never quit. They never say die.

"Let's be honest with ourselves, we got whipped pretty good last week. Did we all want to win? Of course, we did! But men, remember this: the bigger the setback, the greater the comeback. I can't help but wonder if last week's setback happened for a reason. It's the perfect opportunity for each and every one of us to be born again as warriors. To prove to the world — and ourselves — what we're *really* made of. Last week's setback is nothing more than the setup for an epic comeback."

I saw more heads nodding. I felt the energy in the room shifting. They were buying into the message.

"When faced with adversity, a man must make a decision," I said. "He can decide to cower back in disappointment and regret, thinking that it's all just too difficult to go on. That's what most people do. That's what makes them average.

"Or, a man can decide that no matter what he's facing, he will not back down. A man can choose to embrace a warrior's mentality. It takes courage and it takes guts, but most of all it takes relentless grit to become a warrior.

"Who's ready to unleash the warrior inside?" I was raising my voice now. "Who's ready for a comeback? Who's ready to show all the naysayers and everybody who has counted us out that they have no idea what we're about to unleash?!"

I heard some claps, a few shouts, some pounding on desks. The room was about to erupt.

"For the next three weeks, we are going to be relentless in everything we do," I said. "For the next three weeks, we are going to be unstoppable! We are going to attack every day, every obstacle, and every opponent with a level of energy and passion that the college football world has never seen before!"

The energy boiled over and the room exploded with yelling and cheering.

"But remember this," I yelled over the commotion. "It's a choice you have to make. Whether to be a warrior or a quitter is a *choice* that you must make. Each one of you is responsible for that choice. I want to know, right now, who chooses to be a warrior?"

The deafening response gave me the answer I was looking for.

And with that, we entered the final stretch of our season.

22

With a 6-3 overall record, we were 4-1 in the conference and 3-0 in the West Division. This meant that we still controlled our own destiny. If we could win our final three games against West Division opponents, we would win the division and earn a spot in the MAC Championship game.

First up was Central Michigan at home. The Chippewas were 5-4 heading into the game and our largest home crowd of the year welcomed us on this cloudy and extremely windy November afternoon.

Jimmy struggled early in the game, connecting on just one of his first seven pass attempts. That stalled both of our initial drives and Central Michigan capitalized to take a 10-0 lead.

"What's going on?" I asked Jimmy on the sidelines. "Is it the wind?"

"I don't know what it is," he said. "I'm just not feeling it today."

"No problem," I said. "We'll give Ray another shot. Next man up."

Jimmy was surprised by my abrupt decision to replace him, but I couldn't help but think of Bear Bryant's tactics for lighting a fire in his star players by demoting them from time to time. I wanted to see how Jimmy responded.

Ray entered the game and completed his first four pass attempts, leading us to our first touchdown of the day.

On CMU's next drive, Gavin Smith, our senior defensive end, blindsided their quarterback and forced a fumble that we recovered. Ray scored a touchdown on the next play when he tucked the ball and ran it in on a bootleg.

We had another chance to score late in the second half, but Ray overthrew an open receiver and we missed the ensuing field goal attempt in the windy conditions. We went into the locker room with a 14-10 lead at the half.

Jimmy pulled me aside. "Coach, I want back in."

I could see in his eyes that he was furious for getting benched the entire second quarter.

"Ray's playing pretty well," I said. "And you're not feeling it today, remember? Don't worry about it, we all have days like this."

I started to walk away and he stopped me.

"Coach, I can do this," he said. "Please give me another shot."

I looked him in the eyes and gave him a smile. "That's what I like to hear."

Jimmy was a different quarterback in the second half. Though I still swapped in Ray at times to give Central Michigan a different look, Jimmy had taken control of the game. He ended up throwing four second-half touchdown passes as we pulled away from the Chippewas and won the game 48-24.

The following week, we faced one of the top teams in the division as we traveled to Western Michigan on a clear, bitter-cold night in the Upper Midwest. Like us, the Broncos had a 7-3 record and were fighting for a shot at the division title.

Once again, we fell behind early in the game. At halftime, we were trailing 21-13.

Braxton challenged everyone in the locker room to play like a warrior.

"What have we been talking about the last two weeks?" he yelled. "We've got to be unstoppable out there. We've got to be relentless. We've got to be warriors!

"And it all starts up here," he said, pointing to his head. "We've got to *choose* to be unstoppable. It's our choice. Let's choose to play like warriors!"

I couldn't have said it better myself.

It was an even battle in the second half. Western Michigan was a physical and well-coached team. Every time I thought we might be gaining the upper hand, they'd answer with a big play. It was a game that easily could've gone either way, but we kept our focus on only what *we* could control.

With two minutes left to play, we kicked a field goal to take our first lead of the night, 37-35.

But before we could do any celebrating, the Broncos returned the kickoff to midfield. Three plays later, they were inside the 30-yard line. Definitely within field goal range.

They called a few run plays to milk the clock and set their kicker up right in the middle of the field. There was nothing else we could do. We'd played our hearts out, but now it was up to their kicker.

On the last play of the game, he stepped up and booted it high. It looked good as soon as it left his foot. But just as it neared the goal post, it veered off to the right ever so slightly. It banged off the right upright and fell to the turf.

Our players ran onto the field to celebrate with each other. As a coach, I couldn't help but feel bad for the Western Michigan kicker who missed the potential game-winning field goal.

But that's the way this wonderful game goes. I had been on the other side for plenty of heartbreaking endings. You win some and you lose some. All you can do is play *your* absolute best, relentlessly chase *your* dreams, and let the results take care of themselves.

As those thoughts ran through my head, I realized that the beliefs I'd been mentally repeating every day were seeping into my mind and changing the way I viewed the world. They were shaping who I was and the way I was living my life.

At 8-3, we would now be entering our final game of the regular season with the MAC West Division title on the line.

23

The snow had started falling early on the Saturday after Thanksgiving, the day of our final regular season game. But that didn't stop an overflow crowd of more than 30,000 fans from showing up on Saturday night. It was the first sellout crowd at Wisconsin State in more than twenty-five years. It was also Senior Night, the last home game for the seniors on our team.

Toledo entered the game with a 10-1 record and a number 23 national ranking. The Rockets were undefeated in MAC play and they stood atop the West Division. Whoever won this game would represent the West in the MAC Championship game the following week in Detroit.

By game time, several inches of snow had fallen and the windy conditions made it nearly impossible to throw the football. Largely due to three first-half turnovers, we found ourselves trailing 10-0 at the half. And, once again, a gut-check moment at halftime reinvigorated our team.

This time it was Gavin who rallied the troops. Just before heading back onto the field, he yelled, "I've got something to say."

This caught everyone's attention. Gavin was a strong-and-silent type of leader. He led by example and stayed fairly quiet.

"I told you all a couple months back that I almost transferred away from this program," he said. "But I just *knew* I'd regret it if I did. I can't explain exactly how I knew it, but something told me that if we all stuck together we'd find ourselves in a moment like this. With a chance to do something nobody thought we'd be able to do.

"And now, here we are, in my last game *ever* in this stadium. And we're on the verge of winning the division, knocking off *another* school nobody thought we could beat, and *again* turning a setback into a comeback.

"But it's up to us. Right here, right now, it's our decision. Are we going to back down? Are we going to go out there and complain about the cold and the wind and the snow and the bad breaks? Are we going to walk off the field tonight and talk about what we wished we *would've* done or what *could've* happened if conditions had been different?

"Or, are we going to act like the warriors that we are? Are we going to leave every ounce of energy on that field tonight? Are we going to go out there in the wind and the snow and stand up to our opponents and yell, 'Bring it on?' Are we going to choose to be unstoppable for the next thirty minutes of football and break through every wall that stands in our way?!"

The team shouted their resounding answer and nearly took the locker room door off its hinges as they charged back onto the field.

I'm not sure if there's a better feeling for a coach, teacher, or any other type of leader than to hear the message he's been teaching repeated by those he's trying to lead. When the leader can stand back and watch his team lead each other, it's a magical feeling.

We returned the second-half kickoff for a touchdown and could not be stopped from that moment on. The raucous home crowd fed into our energy as we steamrolled through the second half. We were riding a huge wave of momentum that blasted through everything in its way.

Our defense recovered two fumbles in the third quarter and our offense scored touchdowns on each of the short drives that followed.

With a 21-10 lead heading into the fourth quarter, we knew we had Toledo in a tough spot, especially in these snowy conditions where big pass plays were more difficult. Meanwhile, we relied on a steady running game that chewed the clock and kept the chains moving.

When the game ended, we had scored 28 unanswered points to win 28-10 and claim the MAC's West Division title. After three-consecutive come-from-behind victories, we were headed to the MAC Championship game.

Wisconsin State fans stormed the field and our players didn't want to leave. They basked in the joy of this moment, hugging each other and hugging fans.

I didn't want to leave the field either. I found Cindy, who was five-months pregnant, and we embraced as the snow fell.

"I'm so proud of you," she whispered.

"I'm so thankful for you," I said.

It was one of those rare moments where even as it's occurring, you're aware that you don't want it to end. You just want to stay in it and enjoy it for as long as you can.

No matter what happened in the future, this moment was ours. We had been knocked down, we refused to quit, we came from behind again and again, we left everything we had on the field, and we arose victorious.

24

"Don't you think it's about time we discussed your contract?" Larry asked.

My boss had stopped by my office about an hour after the game to coordinate plans for next weekend's MAC Championship. He was now abruptly changing the subject.

"We already had this discussion," I said, not hiding my annoyance that he was bringing it up when I was still trying to enjoy the victory.

He stared at me with a blank expression. "And when did we have this conversation?"

"Well, I guess *we* didn't have it, but I got your message loud and clear."

Larry looked at me like I was speaking in another language.

"A few weeks ago," I said. "And frankly, I still don't understand why you didn't want to tell me your decision face-to-face."

"Chris, I have no idea what you're talking about."

"Before the Bowling Green game. When you told me to meet with Ted Mueller."

"About the fundraising plans for the football facilities?" Larry asked.

Now, I was the one who had no idea what we were talking about. "What fundraising plans?"

At that moment, we both realized what had happened.

"Ted didn't talk to you about those plans, did he?"

"No, he didn't," I said.

"And I assume he instead tried to tell you that your contract would not be renewed?"

"Sure did."

Larry shook his head. "And that's why you've been, well, short with me over the past few weeks, isn't it?"

"He said he spoke for the administration," I said.

"Ted speaks for himself, always has," Larry grumbled. "Let me guess, he told you we were going to hire some old friend of his to be the next coach?"

I nodded.

Larry shook his head again, visibly upset. "He's been trying to get an old high school buddy of his hired for years. The guy he wants may or may not be a good coach, but he's nowhere near qualified. Anyway, that's beside the point. I assure you, we have every intention of offering you a contract extension here at Wisconsin State."

I couldn't believe what I was hearing.

"Then why haven't you brought it up until now?" I asked.

"I figured you didn't want to talk about it. I thought you would find it distracting. Frankly, I wondered if you were feeling out other offers and trying to avoid the discussion."

After a brief moment looking at each other, we both burst out laughing. The feelings of resentment I had towards Larry and the feelings of caution he had towards me over the past few weeks had all been predicated on a lie told by a booster. This gave me yet another reason to never listen to naysayers.

"The day Ted Mueller speaks for this athletic department is the day I no longer work here," Larry said. "Don't get me wrong, I appreciate his passion for Wisconsin State and his father has always been a crucial donor for our program, but Ted's always been, well, a bit of an ass. Nobody around here takes him too seriously."

"I can't tell you how glad I am to hear you say that," I said with a grin.

Larry's tone turned more serious. "Chris, I don't know if you've had any outside offers up to this point, but all I ask is that you give us the chance to meet or beat them. I've watched closely what you've done with the team this year and something special has happened, on and off the field. I've seen a shift that I can't quite explain. Whatever it is, I can see that we're heading in the direction we all want to keep moving in. We are committed to doing everything we can to keep you here at Wisconsin State."

"Thank you, Larry, I really appreciate that." After all I had been through over the past three years, hearing Larry express his gratitude and support for me was almost overwhelming.

"I've been talking with our administration and boosters for the past several weeks," Larry said. "I think we can put together a package that would make you the highest paid coach in the MAC. I'm *certain* I can sell everyone on it if you win the conference championship next week.

"And Chris," he continued, "I actually *do* speak for the administration."

When I got home, I told Cindy everything. About the conversation I'd had with Ted several weeks ago, about my plan to resign shortly afterwards, and about the news from Larry tonight.

"I wish you would've told me about that jerk claiming you wouldn't be back next year," she said.

"I didn't want to burden you with another worry."

"But we're a team. It's easier to shoulder these things when we're in it together."

I was lucky to have a wife and best friend like Cindy.

"Does this mean we're going to stay here?" she asked.

"Yes, it does," I said.

Cindy leapt into my arms and squeezed me tight. She'd been waiting to hear this news for a long time.

At that moment, my cell phone buzzed. It was my agent calling.

"That was fast," I said to Cindy. "Larry must already be presenting a new offer."

I answered and my agent immediately asked, "Are you ready for some big news?"

"Sure am," I said.

"Illinois called. They want to interview you. I told them not to jerk us around. They said they've done the homework and the interview is only a formality. They want to offer you the head coaching job."

I was speechless.

"A Power Five program!" my agent shouted. "And that means Power Five money. We are back in the big leagues, baby!"

Cindy looked at me with misty eyes, waiting to hear about the Wisconsin State contract extension she hoped I was being offered at the moment.

"What kind of money are we talking about?" I asked my agent.

25

Cindy tried, but couldn't hide her disappointment about the offer from Illinois.

"It's not official," I said. "But it sounds good. Really good. I like it here too, but there's just no way a MAC school can compete with an offer from a Big Ten school."

"I understand," she said. "And I'm so proud of you. But I can't help it if my heart wants us to stay here, even if it means less money. There's more to life than money and this place...this place has become our home. This is where I want to raise our family."

"In a year or two, Illinois will feel like home too," I said. "You'll see."

I could tell she didn't appreciate my condescending tone.

"Promise me you'll at least listen to Larry's offer before deciding," she said.

I agreed and we called it a night.

A few hours later, I woke up and was too excited to fall back asleep. I made my way down to the kitchen to hunt for a late-night snack. There, I heard noises coming from our basement. It sounded like a group of people talking and laughing, with music playing in the background.

Our basement was an unfinished space we used mainly for storage. I wondered if a few teenagers had broken into our house thinking no one was home and that they could use our abandoned basement for an impromptu party space.

I grabbed a baseball bat, opened the basement door, and cautiously walked down the steps.

The music and the laughs were much louder. Whoever was in my basement was having a great time.

As I made my way down the steps, I noticed carpeting on the floor. At the bottom of the steps, I found myself in a low-ceilinged, wood-paneled rec room. This was *not* my basement.

The partygoers were adults, dressed mostly in clothes from the 1960s. They were laughing, eating snacks, and clinking their glasses together. There were at least two dozen people here and it took me a moment to recognize any of them.

I followed the jazz music to a stereo in the corner. The man closest to the record player was…Buck O'Neil. He was pointing to a record sleeve in his hands and having a conversation with…Bear Bryant. I smiled, wondering if Buck was winning the Bear over on the merits of jazz music.

Bear was nodding and seemed genuinely interested in what he was hearing.

I saw John Wooden leaning against the far wall, holding hands with the woman I'm sure was his wife and listening intently to whatever it was she was saying as they conversed with another couple. Coach Wooden was too enamored with his wife to notice me.

Sitting in front of the TV on one end of the room was Herb Brooks. He was watching a hockey game. *Intensely* watching it, I might add.

The rest of the people I didn't recognize and they didn't notice me. They were all visiting, laughing, eating, and drinking. Celebrating something, it seemed.

My scan across the room finally took me to the corner bar. Standing beside the bar was the one person who *did* seem to notice me. Smiling big and raising his glass towards me was the unmistakable legend, Vince Lombardi.

26

I dodged my way through the partygoers and made my way to the bar.

"Chris McNeely, congratulations on the big win tonight," Lombardi said in his booming voice. Everything about him was big and forceful—his grin, his voice, his laugh, his barrel chest, his entire presence.

"Thanks, Coach." I looked around the place one more time. It was a time capsule of what basement rec rooms must have looked like in the 1960s. "Can I ask you what you did to my basement?"

"This is my basement," he said. "After every home game, I've always thrown a little party for my friends and family. It's a great way to unwind with the people who are closest to me. This party has grown a bit over the last forty years or so, we're running out of room down here."

"I can see that," I said. "So, Coach, what is it I'm doing wrong?"

"I beg your pardon?" Lombardi said.

"I'm thrilled to meet you," I said. "Like every other football coach in America, I've dreamed of meeting you. But experience has taught me that each time one of you legends shows up for a chat with me, it's because I'm doing something wrong and need to be taught a lesson."

Lombardi roared with laughter. "You're a quick study. I like that. And you don't waste time. I *really* like that!"

I nodded, knowing full well that Lombardi had a reputation for being someone who didn't like to waste even a minute of his time.

"Let's get to it then," Lombardi said. "You've learned some important things from my friends these past few months. Bear taught you the importance of mental toughness and never giving up. Like him, I was probably best known for how much I stressed mental toughness, perseverance, and total commitment in the face of adversity.

"Herb taught you the power of dreaming big, aiming higher than most people dare to aim, and pushing yourself to be the best you can possibly be. He also taught you to ignore the critics, the cynics, and the naysayers. Outstanding advice. I agree with him completely.

"Buck taught you how important it is to love what you do and to tackle each day with a positive, can-do attitude. Again, this is something I totally agree with.

"And Coach Wooden taught you to focus less on wins and losses and instead keep your focus on what *you* can completely control: your effort and your attitude. Give your best and then let the results take care of themselves. Powerful advice to live by. I agree 100 percent with Coach Wooden."

I held up my hand to stop Lombardi. "I have to say, I'm a little surprised to hear you say that."

"Oh, and why's that?" Lombardi asked, a bit defensive.

"Aren't you the one who said, 'Winning isn't everything, it's the only thing?'"

Lombardi shook his head and scoffed. "I've never been able to live that down, have I?"

"It's your most famous quote," I said.

"And I wish to hell I'd never said it. The quote is a little bit out of context. What I said was that winning is not everything, but making *the effort* to win is. I was trying to say that the *will* to win is everything. I meant that giving everything you've got to achieve a worthy goal is what's most important. I sure as hell didn't mean people should crush human values or do immoral things to win.

"In fact, I also said, on many occasions, that the *will* to win and the *will* to excel are more important than the results that follow. Anyone who knows me knows that's what I believe. And I'll always stand by that belief. Man must not ever lose his will to excel and improve. That's the point I've always tried to make, that you can never be apathetic or complacent. You have to keep striving, keep moving forward, keep excelling, and chasing new goals.

"When it comes to winning and losing, I believe that while you can't always be first, you have to believe that you *should* have been first. You must believe that you were never beaten, but that time simply ran out on you.

"Understood this way, I think Wooden and I are in complete agreement on this matter. Wouldn't you agree?"

"Absolutely," I said.

"Good," Lombardi clapped. "Let's move on."

It struck me that the rest of the room was oblivious to the conversation Coach Lombardi and I were having. Either they didn't see me or they knew I was in Lombardi's hands now and they didn't need to assist. I, on the other hand, hung on every one of Lombardi's words.

"What you've learned from the other coaches are four of the five core beliefs that make a champion a champion," he said. "If you—or anyone else—were to embrace these beliefs, to really *live* by these principles day in and day out, you would accomplish anything you set your mind to.

"But there's a fifth belief that needs to be a part of this mindset, one more principle that you need to embrace in your soul. This is the final, and most important, belief."

I leaned forward, eager to hear what this legend was about to tell me.

"A man will only rise as high as his confidence level," Lombardi said with a grin, as though he had just let me in on an extraordinary secret. "And confidence is all about how you approach the unknowable."

He paused for a moment, letting me think about what he was saying.

"There are many things in life that we can't control and we can't know," Lombardi continued. "Each of us must determine exactly how we approach this unknowable realm of life.

"Many people approach this realm with fear and extreme caution. Some people try to ignore this realm, but that strategy usually leads to either too much caution or too much apathy. Champions, however, approach the unknowable realm with *confidence* and *faith*.

"Whether you walk into the unknown with faith or fear determines your future."

He leaned back and again let me absorb what he was saying.

"Every action you take and every decision you make is done out of either faith or fear," Lombardi said. "It's a choice we're all constantly making, usually without even realizing it. Are you walking forward in faith or fear? The answer will determine your success.

"Man will only go as far as his faith and confidence takes him. My job as a coach, a teacher, and a leader was to continuously build more and more confidence in my players. They had to believe they could do more. They had to have faith in themselves and their abilities and this faith needed to be expanded further and further.

"That's the only way to be successful. You defeat defeatism with confidence. The more confidence you have, the more faith you have, the more you believe in yourself and your abilities; the more success and happiness you will have in life.

"The thing is, as I'm sure you know, confidence is a fickle thing. Fear has a way of creeping in and deflating our confidence. Once that happens, you're in big trouble because it spreads defeatism everywhere. A team that thinks it's going to lose is going to lose. Period. Confidence is contagious, but so is a lack of confidence."

"I know that all too well," I said. "Just a few weeks ago, I let one guy's comments make me question everything about my ability. It took a conversation with Bear Bryant to knock me back on track."

Lombardi nodded. "I can relate. Everyone can. Right now, only hours after the big win your team pulled off, fear is creeping back into the psyche of your players. They know what lies ahead. They see a rematch with Bowling Green facing them and they remember a team that beat them by four touchdowns only three weeks ago. This fear is already chipping away at the confidence your players have been building up. You're going to have to reverse this trend as soon as you can."

I now understood why Lombardi was here talking with me. I had overestimated our team's confidence level after the past three victories.

"Sometimes, we start losing our confidence and we don't know why," Lombardi continued. "That's the most frustrating. Regardless of why it happens, the key is to realize that confidence is a precious commodity. It must be continuously protected and built upon. It's the energy that drives you forward and determines your future."

"And how does one do that?" I asked. "How do we make sure we're always building confidence and protecting it? How do we trust that it's safe to choose faith over fear?"

Lombardi smiled big. "I was hoping you would ask that.

"The fastest and easiest way to build confidence is through preparation. If a man knows that he's put in the work and the study and made the sacrifices necessary to be successful at something, he can be confident that he has a huge advantage over those who were not willing to pay such a price.

"For a man to be confident in a task, he must know that he has done everything possible to properly prepare for it. He will then exude confidence.

"Another way to increase confidence is to raise the bar of expectations for yourself and your team. The other coaches talked to you a lot about this, but it bears repeating here. If you refuse to settle for anything less than your best, you'll be amazed at what you can accomplish. Most people set the bar for what they think they can achieve way too low.

"If you want to raise confidence, raise expectations."

"Simple enough," I said.

"Simple, yes. But not always easy, is it?"

"No, it's not."

"Studying people who have already done what you wish to do is another way to quickly and easily build confidence. If they accomplished something you seek to accomplish, simply do what they did and there's no reason you shouldn't be able to accomplish the same. Learn from those who have gone before you, learn how they did it, learn from both their successes and their failures. This is another simple way to build confidence, but most people don't think to do the simple things that lead to success.

"From a leader's perspective, he can quickly build confidence in his troops by letting them know that he believes in them. Again, simple but effective. Of course, the troops must trust the leader for this to be effective and the leader must fully believe what he's telling his troops. You can't fake it.

"Everyone needs to have someone they trust telling them they believe in them. And the most important person who can tell you this is you. You have to tell yourself again and again that you have what it takes to succeed. There is tremendous power in self-talk and the right self-talk quickly produces self-confidence. Always tell yourself that you can do it. Never talk down to yourself. This is an important one. Make sure you understand how powerful self-talk is."

Lombardi looked at me intensely, wanting me to confirm that I understood. I nodded.

"You must also make it a habit of visualizing your future success," he continued. "Use your imagination to see yourself achieving your dreams. Take some time to dream vividly and think about what it will look and feel like when you accomplish your goals. Most people do the opposite. They visualize all the things that could go wrong in the future or have gone wrong in the past. They then make decisions out of fear and a lack of confidence.

"The fastest way to lose confidence is to dwell on past mistakes. Once an error is made, learn from it, then put it out of your mind. The mistake has served its purpose, now it must be forgotten. If you dwell on the mistake, you'll create new fears in your mind. And fear is the enemy of confidence and faith."

"What about overconfidence?" I asked. "When I look back on my time in the NFL, I think my overconfidence led me to horrible results."

"As Herb already told you, there's a difference between overconfidence and arrogance. There's a difference between being self-confident and being irresponsibly egotistical. Egotism stems from fear. Fear that you could be wrong, fear of not wanting to face the truth, fear of failing, fear of losing what you have. A man builds up a false confidence, a false ego, to try to protect himself from all these fears. Sound familiar when you reflect on how you behaved while coaching in Miami?"

I looked down, embarrassed by the way I'd treated coaches, friends, players, bosses, and fans during my time with the Dolphins.

"No reason to dwell on past mistakes," Lombardi snapped. "The point is to learn from those mistakes. Recognize that you crossed a line that shouldn't be crossed. There's a precious balance between being confident and humbly recognizing when you need help from others. Every man knows in his soul when he crosses that line."

"I definitely crossed that line," I said.

"And now you're moving on, better off than you ever were before. It's time to become the person you were born to become. It's time to achieve greatness. A man can be as great as he wants to be if he has *sincere* confidence, courage, determination, and faith.

"It starts with always choosing faith over fear. Everything *will* work out for the best if you make it a habit of choosing faith over fear."

"That's something I struggle with," I said. "I want to have faith that everything will work out, but that's not the way the world always works. Every day, I fear that any success I'm having will be pulled out from under me. It happened before and I constantly fear that it will happen again."

Lombardi looked down and nodded softly, as though he knew exactly what I was talking about.

"I'm going to tell you something that may be a little unpopular to talk about these days," he said in a serious, almost soft-spoken tone. "But it's the honest truth. The source of my faith and confidence has always been rooted in something even more powerful than the things we've already talked about. Without this source, I wouldn't have accomplished a thing."

Before he told me, I knew what he was talking about.

"My faith in a higher power, my faith in God, has always been the center of my life and the source of my strength and confidence," Lombardi said. "The higher power that resides in the realm outside of what we can see and touch, *this* is where I found my confidence. I don't know where else a man could ever find the type of faith I'm talking about.

"In God is where I find my assurance that everything will work out for those who give their very best. I firmly believe that. I have total confidence and total trust in that. God is the greatest source of confidence.

"You see, when we place our dependence on God, we no longer have to worry. This type of faith allows us to be bold, even *recklessly* bold, in the pursuit of our dreams. Faith in God takes confidence to a whole new level. It provides us with help along the way as well as sureness in our action. We can know *with certainty* that if we give our absolute best, God will take care of the rest.

"When you have that type of faith, there is *nothing* to fear. There is no match for this type of confidence."

"I would love to have that type of faith," I said. "But what do you to say to those who point out that sometimes your best isn't good enough and sometimes things don't work out?"

"I'm glad you asked that," Lombardi said quickly, as though he had fielded this question many times. "First off, 'your best' is a rather subjective phrase. Many people who claim they've given their best have actually given far less. They tend to minimize the 'do your best' part of the equation and maximize the 'let God take care of the rest' part. It doesn't work like that.

"I believe we all have a moral obligation to use the talents God has given us and to pursue the dreams God has placed in our hearts. And that means working extremely hard to enhance those talents and chase those dreams. We must see ourselves as co-creators with *the* Creator.

"You see, our skills can only be honed and our character can only be improved by pushing ourselves to the max. By overcoming the struggle and adversity that comes from trying to become the very best we can possibly be. By reaching our limit and then pushing even further. That is how we give our best. That is how we achieve greatness.

"If you give anything less than your best, you're not only cheating yourself, you're also cheating your Maker. You have a responsibility to become the best version of yourself, the person God made you to be. Too many people back down or quit before they give their all."

The look on my face told Lombardi I wanted more.

"I'm not dodging your question," he said. "That's the truth. Most people don't understand what it means to give their very best. They may hope and pray and call that faith, but all along God is waiting for them to get off the couch and start boldly pursuing what it is they desire.

"And don't misunderstand me, I know the importance of prayer. Prayer was central to my life. I went to Mass every morning and I prayed throughout each day. But I never expected those prayers to replace the need for bold and aggressive action on my part. On the contrary, the two were intertwined. My habit of prayer was part of who I was and my faith was the fuel for everything I did. I prayed for guidance and strength and for God to take care of the things that I couldn't. I knew that God expected me to be the best I could possibly be and *then* he would handle the rest."

"But what if someone has genuinely given their best and they still feel things didn't work out for them?" I asked. "We all experience defeat in various aspects of life. That's what makes it so hard to trust a higher power."

"To that I would say, the story isn't finished," Lombardi said. "You're only seeing a small chapter or scene in a much bigger story that God is moving you along in.

"People are constantly being guided down a different path than they originally set out on. I believe the Good Lord tends to put us in the right place. We have to trust that. We have to trust that God knows our purpose better than we do. That requires humility and it's not easy.

"We also have to be careful not to confuse a temporary problem with a permanent one. God has a way of molding us into the people we're supposed to become and often times when we think we've reached the end of the road, it's simply a new beginning."

"You sound like a priest," I said.

Lombardi roared with laughter again.

"If I hadn't become a husband and a football coach, I would've become a priest," he said. "I'm certain of that."

"I didn't realize what a big role faith played in your life."

"It was the most important part of my life," Lombardi said. "I used to tell my players that their list of priorities should go in this order: God, family, and the Green Bay Packers. Faith was first. Faith must always be first. It's the foundation of everything in your life and it's the only source of confidence you can rely on *no matter what*."

"This is an area I know I need to work on," I said. "I've always questioned whether it was safe to trust. To trust that everything will work out. To trust that I'm making the right decision. To trust that God is there to help me when I fall."

"That's the fear talking and you must choose faith over fear. It *is* safe to trust. If you do your part, you can be assured that God will do the rest. He'll put you where you need to be."

As the late-night party continued, Lombardi shared some old stories with me. He told me about the classic *Ice Bowl* game, when the Green Bay Packers beat the Dallas Cowboys to win the 1967 NFL Championship game in a wind chill of negative-50 degrees. He told me about some of his favorite players and coaches. A lot of these stories I was already familiar with, but it was amazing to hear the legendary coach retell them.

What was most revealing was when Coach Lombardi shared some of his regrets with me.

"If I had to do it all over again, I think I would have prayed for more patience and understanding," he said.

His hot temper was something he always struggled with.

Lombardi's obsessiveness with football was another area he struggled to balance.

"I preached faith, family, and football — in that order — but sometimes I had trouble prioritizing things this way," Lombardi said. "And that brings me to the main reason you and I are meeting tonight."

I gave him a confused look. "You mean you're not here to warn me that my team needs its confidence rebuilt?"

"That's important, sure, but you have something even more important that you're dealing with. You're facing a big decision and it requires you to step out in either faith or fear. This decision is something that affects your family a great deal."

"You mean the job offer from Illinois?" I asked. "I'm not sure it's much of a decision. The money, the resources, the prestige they have. Wisconsin State just can't compete with those things."

"Is taking the Illinois job what is best for your family?" Lombardi asked.

"In the long run, I think so. There's much more money in it."

"Sounds like fear talking."

"How so?" I asked.

"You *fear* you won't make enough money by staying here, where your family wants to stay. You *fear* that you will be missing out on something better even though you're finding happiness right where you are. Isn't that correct?"

"I hadn't thought about it that way," I said.

"Most of us don't think about the motivating force behind our decisions as we approach the unknowable. We don't realize when we're choosing faith or fear.

"Before making any significant decision or taking any important action, you have to ask yourself, 'Am I doing this based on faith or fear? Am I doing this based on confidence or worry?'

"Remember this: success follows faith and failure follows fear. Make sure you choose faith over fear."

27

I woke up the next morning with my head on the kitchen table.

"Rough night?" Cindy asked with a smile as she started the coffee.

"I'm not sure," I said, foggy and disoriented.

"What's that?" Cindy pointed to my right.

I looked over to see a sheet of paper with words I didn't remember writing. It said:

I CHOOSE FAITH OVER FEAR. I have complete and total confidence that I have what it takes to accomplish the dreams in my heart. Most failures are a result of people falling to their fears and worries. I am fearless. I am fully committed to pursuing my dreams, developing the unique talents I've been blessed with, and becoming the person I was born to be. I know that if I give my absolute best today, I can safely trust God to put me where I need to be and to make sure that everything works out for the best. I believe I am here for a reason and I have everything I need to fulfill my purpose in life. Success follows faith and I have unbreakable faith.

Cindy could tell by my reaction that I didn't recognize the sheet of paper next to me.

"Are you feeling alright?" she asked.

I quickly folded up the sheet. "I'm fine, there's just something I need to do."

An hour later I was in my office putting together a booklet of the things I had learned from the five coaches who visited me. I knew I *had* to get this booklet into the hands of every player and coach on our team.

These beliefs were not only essential to succeeding in football, they were essential to succeeding in life itself.

When our team gathered for the Monday meeting prior to the MAC Championship, I got straight to the point.

"Someone once told me that a man will only rise as high as his confidence level," I said. "On Saturday in Detroit, we have a chance to make history. We have a chance to win this school's first conference championship in almost 30 years. We also have a chance to do something no other team in this program's history has ever done: win *ten* games in one season.

"But, we won't make history until everyone in this room has total confidence that we *will* make history."

I looked around the room and realized Lombardi was right. I saw tension, nervousness, and fear in too many faces.

For the next ten minutes, I told the team everything Lombardi had told me about building confidence and choosing faith over fear.

"The choice is yours," I concluded. "You can choose faith or you can choose fear. But make no mistake about it, the choice is completely up to you. You have the talent; you've proven that time and time again this year. Now, it's up to each of you to convince your mind that you have what it takes to make your dreams come true."

I knew from my conversations with Wooden, Buck, Herb, Bear, and Lombardi what a tremendous feeling it was to realize *you* have the power to control your destiny. This sense of empowerment changes everything.

As I looked around the room, I saw players and coaches who were finally *getting it*. They were taking control of their beliefs. They were taking control of their destinies.

I then passed out a small booklet to every person in the room. On the front cover of the booklet, in big, bold letters, it read: *THINK LIKE A WARRIOR*.

Underneath this title, it read: *The Five Inner Beliefs That Make You Unstoppable*.

And at the bottom of the cover page, it read, in smaller print: *Property of a Wisconsin State WARRIOR*.

The booklet contained just five pages.

I FOCUS ON ONLY THE THINGS I HAVE TOTAL CONTROL OVER: MY EFFORT AND MY ATTITUDE.

By focusing on only what I can control, my effort and my attitude in the present moment, I will have the peace of mind that comes from knowing the results will take care of themselves. I will not lose myself in the past or worry about the future. I will focus on the present. If I truly give my maximum effort to be the best that I can be today, I will be successful. NOTHING can take that from me.

I LOVE WHAT I DO
AND I ATTACK EACH DAY WITH
JOY AND ENTHUSIASM.

I am passionate about what I do for a living. I'm grateful for the talents and interests I've been uniquely blessed with; they lead me to my purpose in life. I am fully committed to doing something I love and something I was born to do. I do not wait for someone to hand me the life I want to live, I go out and create it on my own. My passion for what I do gives me a competitive advantage over those who don't have the same level of passion. I zap negative thoughts and focus on the positive. I find opportunities in every obstacle. Life is good. I am grateful for all the wonderful blessings in my life.

Page 3:

I DREAM BIG
AND I IGNORE THE NAYSAYERS.

I set huge goals and I fully commit myself to achieving those goals. I ignore those who tell me to be more "realistic" about my goals. Naysayers represent the voices of fear and cynicism and I will not listen to them. I remind myself of all the reasons my dreams CAN come true. I will become the best version of myself and the only way to reach my full potential is to aim as high as possible. Every day, a person makes the choice to either move forward or backward. Today, I choose to move forward and chase my biggest dreams. Miracles will occur when I work hard to follow MY dreams.

I AM RELENTLESS AND I WILL NEVER GIVE UP ON MY DREAMS.

I know that problems will come my way, but I know that I have what it takes to overcome each and every one of them. No matter what obstacles I face today, I will fight my way through them. Nothing can stop me from reaching my chosen destination. I CHOOSE to persevere and never back down from the obstacles that stand between me and my dreams. Simply making this decision to never give up ASSURES me of success in whatever I set out to do. I will never, ever give up on my dreams. I am unstoppable.

I CHOOSE FAITH OVER FEAR.

I have complete and total confidence that I have what it takes to accomplish the dreams in my heart. Most failures are a result of people falling to their fears and worries. I am fearless. I am fully committed to pursuing my dreams, developing the unique talents I've been blessed with, and becoming the person I was born to be. I know that if I give my absolute best today, I can safely trust God to put me where I need to be and to make sure that everything works out for the best. I believe I am here for a reason and I have everything I need to fulfill my purpose in life. Success follows faith and I have unbreakable faith.

Tucked inside the booklet was a small card titled, *Think Like A Warrior*. It contained the five inner beliefs:

1. I focus on only the things I have total control over: my effort and my attitude.

2. I love what I do and I attack each day with joy and enthusiasm.

3. I dream big and I ignore the naysayers.

4. I am relentless and I will NEVER give up on my dreams.

5. I choose faith over fear.

"I want you all to start each morning reading every word of this little booklet," I told the team. "And each night, before you fall asleep, read it again. Read it slowly. Sit with each page for a minute or two. Let these beliefs seep into your soul. Let them become second-nature to you. Let them guide the way you think.

"As for the little card inside, carry it with you wherever you go. I want you to get in the habit of pulling out that card and repeating the five beliefs over and over throughout the day. Eventually, they'll be committed to your memory. But for now, you need to hammer these principles home by reading them over and over again.

"Do this before practice. Do it before a test. Do it before a night out with friends. Do it before calling home to your parents. Do it before asking out a girl you like. Do it before making a big decision. Do it before making a small decision. Do it even when you're bored and not sure what you should be thinking about.

"These beliefs need to become a part of who you are. I'm here to tell you, they will change your life. They will make you become the person you were born to be.

"Men, these five beliefs represent what it means to think like a warrior. And warriors are unstoppable.

"If you embrace and live by these five beliefs, *you'll* be unstoppable and you'll accomplish anything you put your mind to."

28

On Saturday in Detroit, we made history.

It wasn't a flawless game. It didn't come easy. We didn't catch all the breaks. We once again had to battle our way back from an early deficit.

But just four weeks after the Bowling Green Falcons had defeated us by 28 points, we returned the favor and beat the Falcons 42-35.

The win gave us Wisconsin State's first MAC Championship since 1988. It also gave the school its first ten-win season ever.

The next morning, Larry offered me a seven-year contract that would make me the top-paid coach in the MAC. It also allowed me to give all my assistants significant raises.

The salary was well short of what Illinois was offering, but when I looked into Cindy's eyes, I knew I wanted to accept Larry's deal and stay at Wisconsin State.

Some people told me I was nuts to pass up on a Big Ten job, but like Coach Lombardi had told me about priorities:

it should go Faith, Family, and *then* Football (or any other career).

What was best for my family didn't necessarily mean chasing the bigger paycheck. So what if that didn't fit in with what the outside world thought I should do? Who cares what the outsiders, the critics, and the naysayers think? I knew what would make *us* happy. My dream wasn't the same as anybody else's. Wisconsin State was my dream now.

The icing on the cake is that we went down to the Boca Raton Bowl three weeks later to face Marshall University, the winner of Conference-USA. Once again we were the underdogs and once again we came from behind to pull off the upset, defeating the Thundering Herd 55-52 in a triple-overtime thriller. In the final game of his football career, Ray scored the winning touchdown. It was on a trick play where I had both quarterbacks in the game and Jimmy threw a pass to Ray.

After the victory, walking off the field, Ted Mueller strolled up beside me, slapped me on the back, and said, "Coach, I never doubted you for a second. I know a winner when I see one and you, sir, are a winner."

All I could do was shake my head and say, "Thanks Ted, I never doubted your support for me." I don't think he realized I was being sarcastic.

We finished the historic season with an 11-3 record and we were ranked number 22 in the final rankings. I was even named the MAC's Coach of the Year.

In the spring that followed our record-breaking season, my son was born and Braxton Tatum was drafted into the NFL. I suppose it was ironically appropriate that the team that drafted Braxton was the Miami Dolphins. I now had to bury my resentment for the organization that fired me and become the team's biggest fan. The selection made Braxton the first Wisconsin State Warrior to be drafted on Day 1 of the NFL Draft in nineteen years.

I was with Braxton during the draft. As soon as his name was called, we hugged and he told me, "Coach, I'm going to read the book you gave us every day and I'm going to carry that card with me everywhere I go. I will never stop thinking like a *Warrior*."

I could not have been prouder.

More important than the wins and the accolades was the fact that I knew my life, and the lives of the players and coaches who had bought into the five beliefs, would never be the same again.

Thanks to the legends who visited me and the beliefs they taught me to embrace, I had a new outlook on life. I would never again let myself fall into a victim mentality.

Instead, I would choose my destiny by choosing my mindset.

I knew there would be plenty of ups and downs in my future, plenty of new opportunities and unforeseen challenges. That's just how life is. But I now understood that how I chose to respond to these ever-changing aspects of life was completely up to me.

I knew that choosing to embrace the five beliefs on that little card would assure me that I could overcome whatever came my way in the future.

From this point forward, I would think like a Warrior. And Warriors are unstoppable.

Bibliography & Recommended Resources

JOHN WOODEN

Wooden: A Lifetime of Observations and Reflections On and Off the Court by John Wooden with Steve Jamison

My Personal Best: Life Lessons from an All-American Journey by John Wooden with Steve Jamison

John Wooden: Values, Victory, and Peace of Mind – A film by Eli Brown

BUCK O'NEIL

I Was Right on Time: My Journey from the Negro Leagues to the Majors by Buck O'Neil with Steve Wulf and David Conrads

The Soul of Baseball: A Road Trip Through Buck O'Neil's America by Joe Posnanski

Baseball – A film by Ken Burns

HERB BROOKS

America's Coach: Life Lessons & Wisdom for Gold Medal Success by Ross Bernstein

Do You Believe in Miracles? The Story of the 1980 U.S. Hockey Team – A film by HBO Sports

BEAR BRYANT

The Junction Boys: How Ten Days in Hell with Bear Bryant Forged a Championship Team by Jim Dent

The Last Coach: A Life of Paul "Bear" Bryant by Allen Barra

Bear Bryant on Leadership: Life Lessons from a Six-Time National Championship Coach by Pat Williams with Tommy Ford

VINCE LOMBARDI

When Pride Still Mattered: A Life of Vince Lombardi by David Maraniss

What it Takes to be #1: Vince Lombardi on Leadership by Vince Lombardi, Jr.

Run to Daylight: Vince Lombardi's Diary of One Week with the Green Bay Packers by Vince Lombardi with W. C. Heinz

About the Author

DARRIN DONNELLY is a fulltime writer and entrepreneur. He and his products have been featured in publications such as *The Wall Street Journal*, *Sports Illustrated*, *Fast Company Magazine*, and newspapers, websites, and radio outlets all over the world. He lives in Kansas City with his wife and three children.

Donnelly can be reached at SportsForTheSoul.com or on Twitter: @DarrinDonnelly.

Collect all 5 books in the Sports for the Soul series...

Visit SportsForTheSoul.com

Old School Grit

An old-school college basketball coach enters the final NCAA tournament of his legendary career and uses his last days as a coach to write letters to the next generation revealing his rules for a happy and successful life: the 15 rules of grit. Consider this book an instruction manual for getting back to the values that truly lead to success and developing the type of old school grit that will get you through anything.

Relentless Optimism

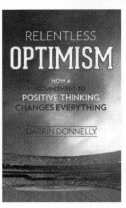

A minor-league baseball player realizes his lifelong dream of making it to the majors is finally coming to an end. That is, until he meets an unconventional manager who teaches him that if he wants to change his outcomes in life, he must first change his attitude. This book will show you just how powerful a positive attitude can be and it will teach you how to use positive thinking to make your biggest dreams come true.

Sports for the Soul Book No. 4

Life to the Fullest

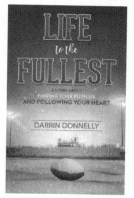

An inspirational high school football fable that pays homage to the holiday classics, *It's a Wonderful Life* and *A Christmas Carol*, this is a story about fathers and sons. It's a story about faith, family, and community. Most of all, it's a story about having the courage to follow your heart and live your true purpose.

Sports for the Soul Book No. 5

Victory Favors the Fearless

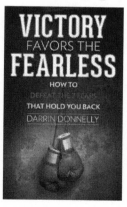

There are seven common fears you must learn to defeat if you want to live a happy and successful life. In this story, a pro boxer learns from a former world champion how to defeat the fears that are holding him back — in the ring and in life. No matter your goal, fear is your ultimate opponent and this book will show you how to defeat the fears that stand between you and the life you were born to live.

Sports for the Soul

This book is part of the *Sports for the Soul* series. For updates on this book, a sneak peek at future books, and a FREE newsletter that delivers powerful advice and inspiration from top coaches, athletes, and sports psychologists, please join us at: **SportsForTheSoul.com**.

Made in the USA
Las Vegas, NV
21 March 2021

19908462R00141